CONTENTS

THE ALL-TIME

CHUBBY ⚾ HOME RUN ⚾ STRIKE OUT ⚾ SWITCH-HITTING
UNDERRATED ⚾ GRACEFUL ⚾ EDIBLE NAMES ⚾ ITALIAN
⚾ SKINNY ⚾ BAD LUCK ⚾ COURAGE ⚾ HANDSOME ⚾ BLACK

BASEBALL
TEAMS
BOOK

THE ALL-TIME

CHUBBY ⚾ HOME RUN ⚾ STRIKE OUT ⚾ SWITCH-HITTING
UNDERRATED ⚾ GRACEFUL ⚾ EDIBLE NAMES ⚾ ITALIAN
⚾ SKINNY ⚾ BAD LUCK ⚾ COURAGE ⚾ HANDSOME ⚾ BLACK

BASEBALL TEAMS BOOK

FRANK COFFEY

St. Martin's Press
New York

This book is for Allison May Coffey, winner

Library of Congress Cataloging in Publication Data
Coffey, Frank.
   The all-time baseball teams book.
    1. Baseball—United States—Miscellanea. I. Title.
GV867.3.C65 1984   796.357′0973   83–23045
ISBN 0–312–02036–8 (pbk.)

First Edition
10 9 8 7 6 5 4 3 2 1

ACKNOWLEDGMENTS

I would particularly like to express my gratitude to Mike Seitzinger, former and, perhaps, future Yankee fan extraordinaire, who read the manuscript and made many comments—some of which were astute. Thanks, Seitz.

My excellent editor, Les Pockell, still a heartsick Brooklyn Dodger fan, made many valuable additions and deletions, though he remains unwilling to believe that "Newk" hit only 15 career homers. His relentless, able assistant, Kathy Babcock, kept us both on track—and her contribution is sincerely appreciated. Leslie Sharpe copyedited the book creatively and enthusiastically; an effort also greatly appreciated.

Jay Acton, my agent, a long-suffering Red Sox fan, told me of various Boston baseball feats—including, in a very short conversation, those of Don Buddin.

Thanks also to my brother Wayne, and friends Raphael Badagliacca, Tom Biracree, Rick Cerrone, Jon Pohlmann, Peter Golenbock, Tom Masucci, and Carl Waldman for their suggestions and comments.

INTRODUCTION

Baseball fans are romantics. For six months a year they live in a world governed by the imagination. Unencumbered by the rules—even the logic—of the all-too-real world, they live those six months believing that their team's hitters will produce crucial base hits in the ninth inning, that their pitchers will strike out the side with the bases loaded, that rookies will fulfill their spring training promise, and that their team will inexorably rise to the league championship and finally to the World Series.

"Ya Gotta Believe" (Tug McGraw's rallying cry for the miraculous 1973 Mets team) is what being a baseball fan is all about. True baseball fans take their game seriously, but know that, in the words of James Taylor, it isn't "really real," but rather a part of a wondrous land called the Imaga-Nation, and meant to be fun.

The All-Time Baseball Teams Book was written in that spirit. On one page you might find The Chubby Team, starring Smokey Burgess, and on the next The Dubious Distinction Team with Mickey Owen. There are statistically valid teams like The R.B.I. Team, and just plain silly teams like The Edible Name Team, which features Eugene Leek at third base. There are controversial teams such as The Overrated Team with Bob Horner, and The Disagreeable Team with Dave Kingman, and even slightly nasty teams like The Unbecoming Team, starring Yogi Berra.

The All-Time Baseball Teams Book is meant to be meandered through rather than devoured. It is a bauble, an entertainment, and should, if I've succeeded, become dog-eared from use—perhaps even spotted with spaghetti sauce, or better yet, hot dog mustard.

In selecting the players for the various teams I have tilted in favor of postwar players, operating on the assumption that the more recognizable the names, the more pleasurable will be the experience of reading the book.

The game has always been a joy for me. I still have my first glove, a 1953 Spalding "Trapper," which today looks too small for anyone to use successfully, including Eddie Gaedel (the legendary midget pinch-hitter). I still fantasize about racing across a perfect green pasture before a screaming, shirt-sleeved crowd to make a game-saving catch. It can happen in the Imaga-Nation.

The All-Time Baseball Teams Book is a fantasy, whimsical, capricious, and, most of all, meant to be fun.

THE ALL-TIME

CHUBBY ⚾ HOME RUN ⚾ STRIKE OUT ⚾ SWITCH-HITTING
UNDERRATED ⚾ GRACEFUL ⚾ EDIBLE NAMES ⚾ ITALIAN
⚾ SKINNY ⚾ BAD LUCK ⚾ COURAGE ⚾ HANDSOME ⚾ BLACK

BASEBALL
TEAMS
BOOK

THE CHUBBY TEAM

P   Mickey Lolich; Freddie Fitzsimmons; Early Wynn
C   Smokey Burgess
1B   Steve Bilko
2B   Don Zimmer
3B   Harmon Killebrew
SS   Honus Wagner
LF   Greg Luzinski
CF   Hack Wilson
RF   Babe Ruth

BENCH: Ed Herrmann; Bob "Fats" Fothergill; Aurelio Lopez; Wilbur Wood; Boog Powell; Rick Reuschel; Terry Forster; Floyd Rayford; Fernando Valenzuela

MANAGER: Tom LaSorda

OWNER: George Steinbrenner

Have you ever tried to locate a chubby shortstop? It's not easy, and an argument could be made that old Honus was stocky, not chubby. Chubby center fielders aren't so easy to come by either. The idea of Hack Wilson patrolling center field must be appalling to purists. On the other hand, every team has to have a center fielder. Hack's elected. (Protests may be mailed to the publisher.) And Honus was five-feet-eleven and weighed 200 pounds. That's chubby in my book. End of argument.

Chubbiest of the chubbies? Smokey Burgess, hands down. When he played for the Pirates, Smokey earned the nickname "the walking laundry bag," which he was said to closely resemble. At the end of his career, rumor has it he tipped the scales at close to 300 pounds. Smokey was, by the way, five-feet-eight inches tall.

Chubbies usually have interesting nicknames. Like "Fat" (Freddie Fitzsimmons), "Bull" (Greg Luzinski), and "Refrigerator" (Steve Bilko). In person, the author advises using their given names.

Baseball record books list Mickey Lolich as six-feet-one and weighing 170 pounds. This is a lie. Appropriately, Mickey, who won 3 games for the Tigers in their 1968 World Series triumph over the Cardinals, today owns a doughnut shop.

Tom LaSorda never met a chocolate eclair he didn't like.

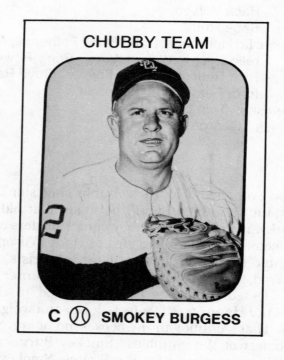

CHUBBY TEAM

C — SMOKEY BURGESS

Ernie Lombardi, a fine catcher primarily with the Cincinnati Reds of the thirties, is second-string all-chubby. Schnozz Lombardi was an aggressive chubby, who regularly refused to chase foul pop-ups that he deemed out of reach, though they landed on the playing surface. Ernie led the league four different times in hitting into double plays. He stole 8 bases in his career, prompting whole-sale firings each time.

The Yankees called their owner, George Steinbrenner, "The Fat Man" during the 1982 season. Steinbrenner responded that he was "hurt" and was "really trying" to lose weight. Anyone who has seen the quantities of hot dogs and ice cream George consumes at the ballpark will wonder just how dedicated a dieter he really is.

My guess is that George will still be first-team all-chubby in the next edition. If so, he will own a fine team; the "chubby" team is one of the best baseball teams in this book.

Did Sidney Greenstreet ever play baseball?

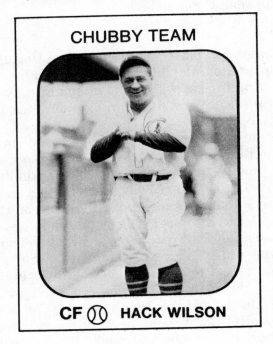

CHUBBY TEAM

CF Ⓧ HACK WILSON

THE SKINNY TEAM

P   Kent Tekulve; Bruce Kison; Ron Guidry
C   Alex Trevino
1B   Enos Cabell
2B   Phil Linz
3B   Felix Mantilla
SS   Bud Harrelson
LF   Ben Oglivie
CF   Omar Moreno
RF   Darrel Thomas
BENCH: Tom "The Blade" Hall; George "Stork" Theodore; Pat Zachary; Gene Stephens; Jim Coates; Mark Belanger; Dick Simpson; Preacher Roe
MANAGER: Connie Mack

By and large, ball players are not skinny. Usually they're just the opposite. After all, they're participating in a fairly sedentary profession with loads of opportunity to snack between meals. (We won't even mention the caloric role played by beer, etc.)

But some people are different. God bless 'em.

In searching for skinnyness, which is not a desirable baseball quality and therefore not easily admitted to by the accused, a sure giveaway is any listing in the club media guide that does not end with a zero or a five. For example, Bruce Kison is listed by the Angels as six-four, 173 pounds. Gotcha Bruce! You might as well announce it over the public address system: I'm thin as a rail. When you've got to fight for every little pound or two, fractions really, it shows how desperate you are.

Darrel Thomas lists his weight as 164. You're not fooling me, Darrel—and, now, none of the readers of this book either. Pretty soon the whole country will know. The truth will out.

Skinny does not, however, mean weak. Don't go pounding on Ben Oglivie's door at night looking for a scuffle. Forget about picking on Enos Cabell or Ron Guidry. Now Bud Harrelson might be a different story. Though, on second thought, he's feisty—he did have a lovely fight with the muscular Pete Rose at Shea Stadium's second base during the 1973 NL Championship Series.

Ever see a picture of Connie Mack? Now that was skinny! Somewhat surprising too, since he certainly could have eaten like a king on the money he saved from paying his players such skimpy salaries.

I think The Chubby Team would beat the stuffing out of The Skinny Team. This opinion is freely given in the hope of fomenting ill will and bad blood among readers. Controversy sells books.

THE OVER-THE-HILL GANG

P   Warren Spahn (23–7)
       Cy Young (22–15)
C   Gabby Hartnett (.300)
1B   Stan Musial (.330)
2B   Nap Lajoie (.280)
3B   Pete Rose (.325)
SS   Honus Wagner (.287)
LF   Ted Williams (.328)
CF   Ty Cobb (.357)
RF   Carl Yastrzemski (.270)
BENCH: Satchel Paige; Jim Katt; Gaylord Perry; Ron Fairly; Early Wynn; Phil Niekro; Hoyt Wilhelm; Bert Campaneris; Willie Stargell; Manny Mota; Lou Brock
MANAGER: Casey Stengel

Despite age, and its concomitant infirmities, The Over-the-Hill Gang is one terrific baseball team. They give everyone with gray hair—or no hair—hope for the future.

Mention of these oldsters brings to mind the first Old-Timers game held by the New York Mets at the old Polo Grounds during their disastrous first season in 1962. (It was noted at the time that the old-timers playing before the regular game were indistinguishable from the current Met players, who were not only the worst team in the league, and probably in history, but also the oldest.) After replaying the legendary Ralph Branca–Bobby Thomson 1951 NL playoff confrontation (Branca got Thomson out on a fly to center this time), the Mets went out and lost 17–0 to the Dodgers.

Hall of Famer Frankie Frisch watched the game, then went home and told his wife: "I don't have to go out of this house again. I've seen everything."

Casey Stengel, age seventy-two, was the manager of that Met team. He is manager of The Over-the-Hill Gang because at sixty-eight he became the oldest manager ever to win a pennant—with the Yankees.

Late in his first season with the Mets, Casey, in an informal session with newspapermen, chose Choo Choo Coleman his "player of the year," describing him as a fellow who "runs very good." At the time, Coleman had been on the team for two days.

Stengel kept using the word "shocked" to describe his Mets, who lost their first 9 games of the year and set a major league record with 120 losses.

Improbably, Warren Spahn, our Over-the-Hill pitcher, played a starring role in the high point of that first Mets' season. In the ninth inning of the first game of a doubleheader, Spahn and the Braves, as usual, were leading the Mets, 2–1. With two outs and a man on first, Hobie Landrith, the woeful Met catcher, (with a .233 career batting average) was up. Hobie swung, misconnected, and launched a weak, 255-foot fly ball into right field. Unfortunately for Spahn, the right-field line at the antiquated Polo Grounds was precisely 254 feet from home plate. The ball landed in the first row of seats for a home run and Spahn was a loser.

After the game, Spahn said, "I want to kill myself."

Oddly, in the second game, Gil Hodges hit an opposite field home run to almost the exact same spot. He hit it in the ninth to break a tie and give the Mets a sweep of the doubleheader.

For the record, Spahn continued pitching, winning 18 games that year at the age of forty-one. The next year, at forty-two, he won 23 games and lost 7, with a remarkable 2.60 ERA. In addition, Spahn pitched two no-hitters—at age thirty-nine and forty!

Great pride was, and is, a common characteristic of the ball players who continue to excel after the age of forty.

Ty Cobb, at an Old-Timers game in 1957, was asked by a reporter what he thought he'd hit if he "were playing today." Cobb thought a moment and said, "About .300." Cobb, whose career batting average was .367, the highest in history, was not known for his modesty. When the surprised reporter asked, "Just .300?" Cobb replied, "Young man, you have to remember I'm seventy-one years old."

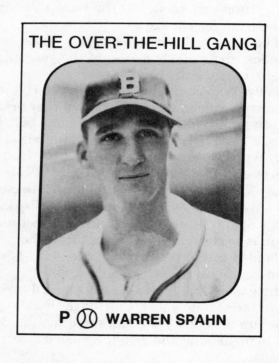

THE OVER-THE-HILL GANG

P Ⓑ WARREN SPAHN

Ted Williams overcame long odds to become a member of The Over-the-Hill Gang. Consider first that Williams lost nearly five years of playing time at the height of his career because of World War II and the Korean War, flying almost eighty combat missions as a jet fighter pilot—enough to age anyone prematurely. Then consider the vast array of injuries that continually plagued him and you have a career that seemed destined to be foreshortened.

Instead, at the age of thirty-nine and forty, he won consecutive batting titles, hitting a remarkable .388 and then a more mortal .328.

Williams, though often difficult for both fans and players to like, was a gutsy, courageous ball player. In 1941, before a doubleheader that would end the season, Williams had a batting average of exactly .400. That mark had not been attained since Billy Terry batted .401 eleven years earlier—and has never been reached since. Instead of sitting out a meaningless doubleheader that had no effect on the pennant race, Williams chose to play. He got 6 hits in 8 at bats, under the fiercest kind of internal pressure, and finished the season with a .406 mark—the highest average in fifty-one years. His 1941 on-base percentage of .551 is the best ever recorded.

A final Williams capper: In his last major league at bat, the "Splendid Splinter" blasted a home run.

Perhaps the most incredible old-timer of them all was Satchel Paige, who did not enter the major leagues until the age of forty-two! He pitched in the majors until the age of forty-eight and compiled an excellent 3.29 ERA.

That record is both a triumph, and, of course, an American tragedy since Paige's greatest years were spent, due to racial bigotry, exclusively in the segregated Negro Leagues.

Today's major league fans have had the pleasure of seeing two of the most productive over-the-hill guys in baseball history: Pete Rose and Carl Yastrzemski. Thanks for the memories.

THE GREAT UNREWARDED
PERFORMANCES TEAM

P   Harvey Haddix; Steve Carlton; Bob Hend-
        ley; Hugh Casey
C   Thurman Munson
1B   George Sisler
2B   Bobby Richardson
3B   George Brett
SS   Ernie Banks
LF   Billy Williams
CF   Richie Ashburn
RF   Babe Herman
CAREER PITCHING AWARDS: Ned Garver; Bob
        Friend; Ted Lyons

On May 26, 1959, Harvey Haddix threw twelve perfect innings against the Milwaukee Braves for the Pirates, retiring 36 hitters in succession. In the thirteenth the Braves scored an unearned run and Harvey lost 1–0. Gee whiz!

On September 19, 1969, Carlton struck out *19* Mets and lost the game 4–3 when he gave up two 2-run homers to Ron Swoboda.

On September 9, 1965, Sandy Koufax pitched a perfect game against the Cubs. His mound opponent, Bob Hendley, pitched a one-hitter, and lost the game 1–0.

Poor Hugh Casey. He did absolutely everything right in the fourth game of the 1941 World Series. With the Dodgers down two games to one to the Yankees, Casey came into the game in the fifth inning with the bases loaded and got the tough Joe Gordon to end the inning. In the top of the ninth with two out, nobody on base, and the Dodgers ahead 4–3, Casey threw a third strike past slugger Tommy Henrich. Catcher Mickey Owen muffed the pitch, Henrich ran to first, and the Yankees rallied to score 4 runs and win 7–4. Ahead three games to one, the Yankees won the Series the next day.

But hold on, fans, here's Casey's revenge. In the 1947 Series, Casey got Henrich to hit into a double play in the eighth inning of the fourth game. Then in the ninth, Cookie Lavagetto broke up the Yankees' Bill Bevens' bid for a no-hitter and Casey was the winning pitcher. (Unfortunately for the Dodgers, the Yanks won the Series in seven games.)

All Thurman Munson did in the 1976 World Series against the Reds was hit .529. The Yanks lost in four straight and Reds' manager Sparky Anderson rubbed salt in Munson's psychic wounds by stating that it would be "embarrassing" to compare any other catcher in baseball to his own Johnny Bench.

In the 1960 World Series, Yankee second baseman Bobby Richardson set an all-time Series record with 12 RBIs, and batted .367. But the Pirates' second baseman, Bill Mazeroski, stole the headlines. His ninth-inning homer won the Series.

George Brett hit an incredible three homers in the third game of the 1978 American League playoffs. But Thurman Munson hit a homer in the eighth to win it for the Yankees, 6–5. On the next day New York took the pennant. Thurman knew how you felt, George. (Extremely small consolation.)

George Sisler played fifteen wondrous seasons, compiling a .340 career average. He hit .400 twice; his 1920 mark of .407 was achieved with 257 hits, still the single-season record. He never played in a World Series; in fact, he only played three seasons on teams that had a better than .500 record, and finished his career with the futile Boston Braves. A truly great player fated to play on truly terrible teams.

Ernie Banks certainly knows how old George felt. Banks pounded 512 career homers, all for the woeful

Cubbies, and never played on a pennant-winner either. Somehow Ernie managed to enjoy himself anyway.

Billy Williams shared many of those disappointing seasons with the Cubs. Billy played eighteen superlative years and appeared in 1,117 consecutive games from 1963 through 1970—which showed that he didn't discourage easily. (His NL iron man record was eclipsed by Steve Garvey in 1983.) Despite 426 career homers and a .290 lifetime batting average, he never played in the World Series or on a pennant-winner either.

Compared to Sisler, Banks, and Williams, Richie Ashburn was flat out lucky. In his third season with the Phillies, 1950, the "Whiz Kids" won the pennant and went to the Series—where they were wiped out by the Yankees 4–0. After 1950 he never played another postseason game. Richie, a career .308 hitter, finished up with the 1962 Mets, a final indignity.

Babe Herman hit .381 for the bad news Brooklyn Dodgers of 1929—and lost the batting title to Lefty O'Doul, who stroked a whopping .398. Babe tried even harder in 1930 and finished with a gorgeous .393. But Billy Terry picked 1930 to hit .401. Herman was a lifetime .324 hitter who never enjoyed a pennant or a batting title.

Career Awards: Ned Garver is the only pitcher in major league history to win 20 games with a club that lost 100 games (Garver, 20–12; the 1951 St. Louis Brownies, 52–102). Poor Ned pitched fourteen big-league seasons and in eleven of them his team finished sixth or worse. In his last five years with Kansas City and the L.A. Angels his teams finished seventh, seventh, seventh, eighth, and eighth. Ned Garver, no doubt, is a man of strong character.

Ted Lyons, Hall of Fame pitcher, won 260 games in twenty-one years with the hapless White Sox. In sixteen of those years the Sox finished below .500.

In Bob Friend's first seven years in the majors with the pathetic Pirates (1951–57), the team finished last four times, and next to last the other three. Friend had to win the National League ERA title to get his first winning percentage in 1955 (14–9). In sixteen years of pitching major league baseball Bob was with one pennant winner (he went 18–12), one second-place finisher (22–14), and one third-place finisher (8–12 but with a respectable 3.24 ERA). The other thirteen seasons were nightmares.

Fittingly, we suppose, he ended his last season, 1966, dividing his time between the ninth-place Mets and the tenth-place Yankees. It ain't right, Bob. It ain't fair.

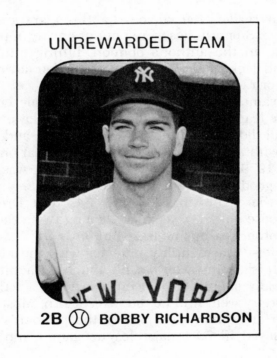

UNREWARDED TEAM

2B ⚾ BOBBY RICHARDSON

THE SLOW TEAM

P   Mickey Lolich; Sparky Lyle
C   Sherm Lollar and Ernie Lombardi (tie)
1B   Walt Dropo
2B   Bob Heise
3B   Harmon Killebrew
SS   Jim Fregosi
LF   Greg Luzinski
CF   Jim Hickman
RF   Frank Howard

Yes, dear reader, the choices for this team are highly subjective. Stopwatches were not put on any of these fellows but, in the author's opinion, hitting into double plays and lack of thefts give a pretty fair idea of foot speed—or rather the lack thereof.

For example, both Sherm Lollar and Ernie Lombardi led their leagues in hitting into double plays. In fact, Lombardi did it four times (1933, '34, '38, and, '44), a record, with a high mark of 30 in 1938. Lollar only did it once, in 1959, but I saw Lollar play and, boy, was he ever slow. In good conscience I had to call it a tie.

With the Tigers in 1953 and '54, Walt Dropo was turned loose on the basepaths, stealing twice each year. In nine other seasons he was shut out.

Bob Heise was a utility infielder with the Mets and seven other teams who wasn't much of a hitter but theoretically should have been able to do all the little things pretty well. And he did, except run. Most second basemen are quick—it's part of the position's profile. Heise played in 500 major league games and stole 3 bases.

Can any third baseman run? Killebrew, who stole 19 bases in 22 years, is our choice here, but there are lots of alternatives.

Greg "The Bull" Luzinski, according to *The Baseball Encyclopedia,* stole 8 bases in 1978. I, for one, am not a believer, and I assume that anyone who has seen Greg play is not a believer either.

Jim Hickman once said he didn't like playing the outfield because he got tired running in and out between innings. I have never heard that one before—or since. Hickman played center field for the Mets in 1963 and '64, appearing in 285 games without stealing a base. Hey, center field is far—Jim had to save his legs on the rare occasions when he did reach base just to be sure he had enough gas in the tank to get out to his position.

Jim Fregosi once stole 17 bases in a season, but by the time he reached the ripe old age of twenty-eight he had apparently discovered pasta. With the 1970 Angels, Jim played 158 games without stealing a base, and for players who appeared in 150 or more games in a season, that's an all-time record.

Big Frank Howard, more often described as "lumbering" than any man in baseball history, stole 8 bases in sixteen big-league seasons, with a personal season-best of 1.

No one has ever seen either Mickey Lolich or Sparky Lyle run one step. Even the *idea* of them running seems ludicrous.

Statistics-Can-Be-Misleading-Department: Hank Aaron holds the career record for grounding into double plays. Yet Aaron ran very well, as his 240 career stolen bases (with a season high of 31) attests.

Statistics-Aren't-Always-Misleading-Department: As a player, ex-Cincinnati manager Russ Nixon played 906 consecutive games over twelve years without stealing a base.

THE FAST TEAM

P	Ron Guidry
C	John Wathan
1B	Rod Carew
2B	Joe Morgan
3B	Jackie Robinson
SS	Maury Wills
LF	Rickey Henderson
CF	Willie Wilson
RF	Lou Brock

BENCH: Willie Davis; Bobby Bonds; Cesar Cedeño; Freddie Patek; Willie Mays; Tommy Harper; Bert Campaneris; Billy North; Omar Moreno; Vada Pinson; Luis Aparicio; Dave Lopes; José Cardenal; Tim Raines.

Fans, please remember this team is tilted completely toward modern players. So many more bases were stolen by everybody fifty years ago that combining modern-day players and old-timers on a team would be difficult, if not impossible, to do fairly.

Before Ron Guidry started winning big in the major leagues the Yankees regularly used him as a pinchrunner. Not any more.

Rod Carew has stolen home an amazing seventeen times in his career. His single season high is 49—no modern first baseman comes anywhere near Rod's basestealing performance.

Joe Morgan is the only man in baseball history to steal 60 bases (or more) and hit over 25 homers in a single season. Joe did it twice in his glory years with the Cincinnati Reds (1973: 67 thefts and 26 round trippers; 1976: 60 stolen bases and 27 homers).

Jackie Robinson led the National League twice in stolen bases; though his season high was "only" 37, anyone who saw Jackie play knows this statistic doesn't do justice to the disruption his daring, hard baserunning caused the opposition.

Maury Wills stole 104 bases in 1962, at age thirty, a record that stood for twelve years until thirty-five-year-old Lou Brock stole 118. Brock's 917 stolen bases is the all-time record. Long may they run.

Rickey Henderson stole 130 bases in 1982, terrorizing the American League and setting a new standard for major league thievery that may never be surpassed.

Willie Wilson has stolen as many as 83 bases in a season and holds the AL record for least double plays hit into in one season (1—1979). There is no one playing today faster than Wilson.

Odd Fact Department: Herb Washington was the only designated runner in major league history—another innovation from the fertile, febrile mind of Charlie Finley. Herb appeared in 104 games for the champion Oakland A's of 1974–75 and never had an at-bat! He stole 30 bases, and was probably very bored most of the time.

THE DUBIOUS DISTINCTION TEAM

P   Bob Moose; Ralph Terry; Ralph Branca
C   Mickey Owen
1B   Gil Hodges
2B   Mike Andrews
3B   Eddie Mathews
SS   Roger Peckinpaugh
LF   Dave Winfield
CF   Gary Maddox
RF   Ted Williams
HONORABLE MENTION: Fred Merkle; Willie Davis; Jack Chesbro; Johnny Pesky; Hank Gowdy; Willie Wilson; Mike Torrez; Mike Schmidt

The array of outstanding ball players on this team makes one realize that bad things happen to us all; it's part of life.

That thought probably wouldn't make Ralph Branca feel any better about Bobby Thomson's "shot heard 'round the world," which won the pennant playoff for the Giants in 1951. You're not alone, Ralph; in fact, pitchers are particularly vulnerable to major mistakes. It's their lot in life to be either complete successes or total failures.

Jack Chesbro won 41 for the 1904 Yankees—the highest total in the twentieth century. He also threw a wild pitch in the ninth inning of the last game of the season against the Red Sox to give the Sox the pennant. Feel better, Ralph?

Bob Moose did the same thing in the ninth inning of the fifth and final game of the 1972 National League Championship Series, giving the pennant to Cincinnati over the Pirates. Ironically, Moose is an excellent control pitcher and walked only 47 batters in 226 innings during 1972.

18

Most people know about Ralph Terry's boo-boo. For those who don't, it was a hanging slider delivered to Bill Mazeroski with two out in the ninth inning of the seventh game of the 1960 World Series. Boom.

Mickey Owen may well be the most famous goat in major league history. A ninth-inning, 2-out, bases-empty strikeout became a 4-run, heartbreaking Yankee rally. Many of Mickey's teammates never forgave him.

The wonderful Gil Hodges, one of the game's finest-fielding first basemen—and true gentlemen—committed a 2-out error in the crucial fifth game of the 1952 Series against the Yankees that allowed Mickey Mantle to bat with the bases loaded. You guessed it, one grand-slam tragedy coming up. Yankees won the next game to take the Series. At the plate, Gil went 0 for 21.

Mike Andrews, Oakland's slick-fielding second baseman, booted two routine grounders in the twelfth inning of Game Two of the 1973 Series, handing the Mets the longest game in World Series history. Subsequently Andrews was both humiliated and cheated by A's owner Charlie Finley, who first tried to have Andrews replaced on the roster by cooking up a phony back injury. Later Andrews discovered that his World Series ring contained a piece of glass, rather than a diamond. Andrews' behavior throughout his ordeal won the admiration of many; Finley's was, at the least, contemptible.

Eddie Mathews set a World Series record by striking out 11 times in the 1958 classic in which the Yankees came back from a 3–1 deficit to win. He hit .160. (Eddie was the hero of the '57 Series, so maybe things really do balance out. And his strikeout record was broken by Willie Wilson, who had 12 Ks in the 1980 Series.)

Roger Peckinpaugh, the American League MVP in 1925, committed an incredible 8 errors in the World Series of that year. One of those errors gave the Pirates Game Two. Two more, in Game Seven, resulted in 4 unearned runs and ended the Senators' season.

Dave Winfield, the Yankees' number-three hitter, batted .154 in the 1981 AL Championship Series and then .045 in the World Series, going 1 for 22. He tied the Series record for fewest runs scored—zero.

Perennial Golden Glove outfielder Gary Maddox messed up by dropping Ron Cey's easy fly ball in the tenth inning of the final game of the 1978 National League Championship Series. Bill Russell followed with a single and the Dodgers defeated the Phillies.

Ted Williams was always stubborn and his Dubious Distinction Award is a tribute to mental attitude as well as physical performance. The AL MVP in 1946 (38 home runs; 123 RBIs; .342 average) was greeted in the 1946 World Series with the St. Louis Cardinals' version of the Boudreau Shift, in which only the left fielder and third baseman remained on the left side of the diamond against the left-handed pull hitter. Instead of simply tapping the ball into left field, Williams tried time and time again to hit directly into the heart of the packed defensive right side of the field. The result: a .200 average, with no extra base hits and 1 RBI. The Red Sox lost in seven games.

Honorable Mention: Roger Craig lost 24 games for the 1962 Mets, the worst performance ever by a pitcher. Craig's most dubious distinction occurred in the *first* inning of the *first* game the Mets ever played when he balked in a run. Now that's an omen if there ever was one.

THE LITERARY TEAM

P   Jim Brosnan (*The Long Season*)
        Jim Bouton (*Ball Four*)
        Sparky Lyle (*The Bronx Zoo*)
C   Joe Garagiola (*Baseball Is a Funny Game*)
1B   Pete Rose (*Charlie Hustle*)
2B   Billy Martin (*Number 1*)
3B   Ron Cey (*Portrait of a Penguin*)
SS   Ernie Banks (*Mr. Cub*)
LF   Lou Brock (*Stealing Is My Game*)
CF   Mickey Mantle (*The Quality of Courage*)
RF   Jimmy Piersall (*Fear Strikes Out*)
MANAGER: Leo Durocher (*Nice Guys Finish Last*)
OWNER: Bill Veeck (*Veeck as in Wreck*)

Okay, let's be frank about this. You and I both know that the vast majority of baseball books are not written by the ball players themselves, but by co-writers or ghost writers. But, gee whiz, we don't have to be sticklers about this, do we? Who's it going to hurt to call Mickey Mantle literary?

Still, I've made an honest attempt—well, partially honest—to include on this team ball players who really and truly contributed to producing a good book. Anyone who's been in or around baseball knows that dumb ball players don't write or dictate or tape-record good books. Only bright, sensitive guys can do that. Really.

In some of the above cases, the ball players did all the writing themselves. I applaud those hearty few. I know only too well what a pain in the neck, butt, and wrists writing can be. It's bad for the eyes too. Worse than movies or even night ball. Who knows how many years

Joe Garagiola lost from his brilliant career because he was squinting at pica type in some lonely hotel room. Decades probably. Maybe more.

On the other hand, some of the fellows included here did no damage to their eyesight. One ball player, author of a highly successful book, once told me after more than a few Scotches, that he couldn't discuss what was in his own autobiography because he hadn't read it. As Kurt Vonnegut would say, "So it goes."

LITERARY TEAM

P ⚾ JIM BROSNAN

Jim Brosnan is clearly *the* writer of our literary group. *The Long Season,* twenty years after being written, is still one of the finest insider's books on baseball ever written: a clear, lucid account of the emotional rollercoaster ride that is each player's life for six months a year.

I had lots of pitchers' books to choose from—since

22

most pitchers work about one in four days, if that. With all their free time pitchers either write books or grow tomatoes in the bullpen. These endeavors are about equally profitable—depending on the size of the tomatoes.

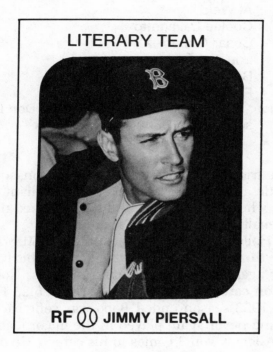

LITERARY TEAM

RF JIMMY PIERSALL

THE BRIEF-MOMENT-IN-THE-SUN TEAM

P   Bobo Holloman; Floyd Giebell
C   Elrod Hendricks
1B   Dick Sisler
2B   Al Weis
3B   Cookie Lavagetto
SS   Cesar Gutierrez
LF   Lou Johnson
CF   Bernie Carbo
RF   Ron Swoboda
BENCH: Dusty Rhodes; Al Gionfriddo; Don Larsen; Bucky Dent; John Paciorek

What we tried to do here was gather "inconsequential" guys, little guys, who experienced one brilliant, shining moment when time stopped and they realized the fantasies baseball fans and players share alike.

Bobo Holloman's moment occurred on May 6, 1953, when he threw the only complete game of his career—a no-hitter against the Philadelphia Athletics. Holloman's one-season career record was 3–7 with a 5.23 ERA. Before the 1953 season ended Bobo was sent back to the minors and never again played in the major leagues.

Floyd Giebell won 3 games in his career. He pitched 2 games in 1940 and the second was a 2–0 shutout victory over mighty Bob Feller that gave the pennant to the Detroit Tigers on the last day of the season. Floyd never won another major league game.

Elrod Hendricks, the longtime Baltimore Oriole backup catcher, was a .220 lifetime hitter who in the 1970 World Series hit .364, tying the first game with a home run, and providing the winning runs in Game Two with a 2-run double. The Orioles went on to swamp the Reds, four games to one. Ellie also threw out two runners trying to steal, made a spectacular tag at home plate, and thoroughly outplayed baseball's best catcher, Johnny Bench, who managed only a .211 batting average.

BRIEF MOMENT TEAM

P BOBO HOLLOMAN

Dick Sisler played eight low-key years with a .276 batting average—64 points lower than his dad, Hall of Famer, George. But Dick's moment in the sun made up for a career spent in the shadows. On the last day of the 1950 National League season the Dodgers and the Phillies were playing for the pennant. With the league's two best pitchers, Robin Roberts and Don Newcombe, locked in a tight battle, the game, tied 1–1, went into the tenth inning. Then, with two men on base, Sisler cracked a home run giving the Phillies their first pennant in fifteen years. George Sisler, the Dodgers' chief scout, sitting in the stands, saw his son's blast end his own team's season.

Al Weis was a classic good-field, no-hit infielder who played ten years and ended up with a .219 average. But in the 1969 World Series Weis hit .455. His 2-out, ninth-inning single won the second game. Then, in the fifth and deciding game, Weis' seventh-inning home run tied the game. Weis hit 7 home runs in his entire career.

In Cookie Lavagetto's final major league season he had 13 RBIs. Two of those RBIs came with 2 out in the ninth inning of Game Four of the 1947 World Series when Cookie doubled to break up Yankee pitcher Bill Bevens' no-hitter. The double went into the right-field corner, the first time Cookie had hit a ball to right the entire season. It was his last major league hit. And Bevens' last major league game.

On June 21, 1970, Cesar Gutierrez, a utility infielder with a lifetime .235 batting average, banged out 7 consecutive hits for the Tigers against the Cleveland Indians. The next year Gutierrez managed 7 hits the entire season, batted .189, and was released, his career at an end.

Lou Johnson was a thirty-one-year-old minor league retread who had not played in the majors for three years when he made the 1965 Dodger team. But Sweet Lou wasn't finished, batting a respectable .259 for the season with 12 homers and 58 RBIs. Then, in the fourth inning of the seventh game of the World Series against the Minnesota Twins, Johnson smacked a home run—giving Sandy Koufax all the runs he needed to win 2–0.

Bernie Carbo never put together one consistent major league season in a career beset by controversy. But in Game Six of the 1975 World Series—the game many label the greatest game in baseball history—Carbo pinch-hit a 3-run, 2-out, eighth-inning home run to tie the score against the mighty Cincinnati Reds, Bernie's old team. Then in the twelfth, Carlton Fisk hit a home run to win it all. Carbo was traded the next year and never again played a full major league season.

Ron Swoboda was a muscular slugger who never hit consistently in the big leagues. No one thought of him as a good outfielder, or even for that matter a decent one. Early in his career he was booed unmercifully for his frequent errors, but Swoboda kept trying and by 1969, his fifth season, he had managed to become a respectable, careful fielder who committed only 2 errors the entire year. Perhaps it was his growing confidence that allowed Swoboda to attempt and make one of the riskiest and greatest catches in World Series history. It was the ninth inning of the fourth game of the '69 Series with the Mets ahead 1–0. With Orioles on first and third and one out, Brooks Robinson hit a sinking line drive to right center. Swoboda raced in, dove full length, and back-handed the ball inches before it hit the ground. If the ball had gotten through, at least 2 runs would have scored. One run did score when Frank Robinson tagged up, but the catch saved the game—which the Mets won in the bottom of the tenth. (Swoboda also hit .400 in the Series.) The Mets won the Series, four games to one, the biggest upset in baseball history.

Dusty Rhodes was a hard-living journeyman ball player (lifetime .253 average) who hit .667 in the '54 World Series, with two game-wining homers and one game-winning single. A pinch-hitter and part-time outfielder, he had a third of his team's RBIs.

Al Gionfriddo made one of the memorable catches in World Series history when he robbed Joe DiMaggio in the sixth inning of the sixth game of the 1947 Series with a spectacular running grab in deep left centerfield. Gionfriddo never played another major league game. At twenty-five he was through, but Al left a memory that thousands of Dodger fans will cherish forever.

Don Larsen was a thoroughly mediocre big league pitcher who two years before he pitched his perfect game in the 1956 World Series had a 3–21 record with a 4.37 ERA. He played for eight major league teams and ended up with an 81–91 record.

Oddest-Brief-Moment-Department: In 1966 John Paciorek (the White Sox Tom's older brother) played one game for the Houston Colt 45's (now the Astros), went 3-for-3, knocked in 3 runs and scored 4. It was the only major league game he ever played in.

BRIEF MOMENT TEAM

Bench 🔘 DON LARSEN

OH BROTHER: THE SIBLING RIVALRY
TEAM

(Statistics given are career totals)

P   Henry Mathewson (0–1)
      Von McDaniel (7–5)
C   George Dickey (.204)
1B Jim Buckner (.000)
2B Hank Allen (.241)
3B George Freese (.257)
SS Pompeyo Davalillo (.293)
LF Jim Nettles (.225)
CF Vince DiMaggio (.249)
RF Tommy Aaron (.229)
BENCH: Calvin Fisk; Ron Allen; Chris Bando; Rich, Charles, Leon and Vince Murray
NOTE: There have been 275 brother combinations in major league history

Unfortunately, some of these statistics will give the reader the impression that the poor brothers listed above were better than they actually were. For example, Hank Allen, brother of slugging Richie (call me "Dick") Allen, managed 6 home runs in seven years of play—placing him exactly 345 homers behind his brother. Tommy Aaron almost doubled that production, hitting 13 homers in seven years, but that still left him 742 homers behind Hank. Oh boy.

Gene Freese was an excellent third baseman in the fifties and sixties who averaged about 10 homers a year. George averaged 1 a year—for a total of 3. Vince DiMaggio, clearly the best player listed above, had a career batting average that was a full 76 points below his brother Joe's. Must have made for a lot of long dinners listening to advice.

George Dickey managed 4 homers to go with his .204 average. His brother Bill did much better.

Christy Mathewson won 373 more games than his brother Henry. In comparison, Von McDaniel's performance was practically the equal of brother Lindy's, lagging only 134 wins behind.

Pompeyo Davalillo, brother of Vic, played in a total of 19 games, all with the utterly hapless Washington Senators. Pompeyo's nickname was Yo-Yo.

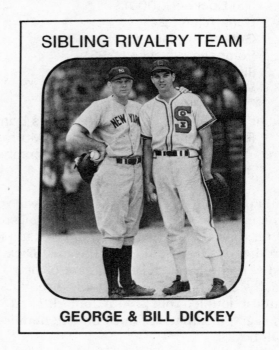

SIBLING RIVALRY TEAM

GEORGE & BILL DICKEY

THE EDIBLE NAME TEAM

P	Edgar Bacon; Arthur Herring; Jacob Munch
C	Johnny Oates
1B	Bennett Rochefort
2B	Chico Salmon
3B	Eugene Leek
SS	Coot Veal
LF	Zack Wheat
CF	Chet Lemon
RF	John Mayo

Honorable Mention: Howard Johnson

BENCH: Beveric Bean; Thornton Kipper; Frank Pears; Bob Moose; Mark Lemongello; Laurin Pepper; Dizzy Trout; Duke Carmel; Ralph Ham; Bobby Sturgeon; Charles Frank; Danny Napoleon; Darryl Strawberry

First: These names are all real. Honest.

Second: This is an awfully silly team. What an author will do for money!

Third: Excepting Wheat and the up-and-coming Strawberry, this is a terrible group of baseball players.

Fourth: Which way to the refrigerator?

THE HOME RUN TEAM

P	Wes Ferrell (38)
	Red Ruffing (37)
	Bob Lemon (37)
C	Johnny Bench (45; 367)
1B	Jimmie Foxx (58; 534)
2B	Rogers Hornsby (42; 302)
3B	Eddie Mathews (47; 512)
SS	Ernie Banks (47; 512)
LF	Hank Aaron (44; 755)
CF	Willie Mays (52; 660)
RF	Babe Ruth (60; 714)

This lineup is enough to make any pitcher develop bursitis or an upset stomach or an ailing parent right before game time. It's horrifying to realize that Johnny Bench or Eddie Mathews would bat eighth on this team.

Wes Ferrell had 9 homers in his best season, 1931, and actually had more career homers than his brother Rick, a catcher, who was a career .300 hitter and went to the plate almost 5,000 more times! Ferrell, Wes, a good pitcher who won 193 big league games, had a career .280 average and actually led the Carolina League in hitting at age forty with a .425 average.

Red Ruffing had a career .269 average, won 273 big league games, and knocked in 273 runs.

More recent power-hitting pitchers include Warren Spahn (35), Don Drysdale (29), Bob Gibson (24), and Milt Pappas (20).

Johnny Bench passed Yogi Berra in the home run parade during 1981; all things considered, Bench is probably the best catcher in baseball history. But to make things interesting, let's all keep an eye on Gary Carter.

Jimmie Foxx edged Gehrig at first base with a better home run ratio (6.6 to 6.2) and 40 more total homers. (Home run ratio is the number of homers per 100 at bats.) Willie Stargell and Willie McCovey, both over 500, were right there too.

No second baseman had anything like Hornsby's power except Joe Morgan (298 career HRs), but his single-season high is "only" 27, a far cry from the Rajah's 42. Davey Johnson hit about half as many home runs as Hornsby, but he belted 43 in 1973—and that's a record; plus a tribute to Atlanta's beneficial home run climate.

Eddie Mathews is the greatest home-run hitting third baseman by a mile. But watch out for Mike Schmidt—he's on the move.

No contest at short, with smiling Ernie Banks completely outdistancing all comers. "But Banks stopped playing short early in his career," you're going to say. Nonsense. Banks was a full-time shortstop until age thirty—eight full seasons—and his best home run year ever—47—was accomplished at short. Even if we were to count only the homers he hit while playing SS exclusively, Ernie's 298 total is way ahead. Today's fans might wonder if Robin Yount—the 1982 AL MVP—has a chance to catch Banks. Not really. Yount didn't reach double figures in homers until 1980 and isn't over 100 after eight seasons.

Most of the great home run hitters had one or more monstrously big seasons, except for Hank Aaron, whose high was "only" 44—the lowest single-season total of the regulars except for Hornsby's 42. But good Lord, was Hank consistent, averaging 36 homers over 21 years!

Willie Mays is third in total career homers and eleventh in HR ratio with 6.1, despite playing in one of the worst home run parks (Candlestick) for fourteen years. Backing up Hank and Willie is Mickey Mantle, whose 6.6 HR ratio topped them both, though his 536 total is significantly lower.

Babe Ruth, it is instructive to remember, has by far the highest home run ratio in history at 8.5. The runner-up is Ralph Kiner at 7.1, which means that Ruth averaged, if we assume 500 at bats a season, 7 *more* homers than his closest competitor. And 12 more than Aaron. And 14 more than Reggie Jackson. Ruth was and is the greatest home run threat in baseball history, a man so far ahead of his time that fifty years after he last played, no one has come close to equaling his accomplishments.

Oddest Career Home Run Performance: one John Miller hit a home run in his first major league at bat (1966) and another in his last major league at bat (1969). They were the only home runs he ever hit in the big leagues.

HOME RUN TEAM

1B JIMMIE FOXX

THE STRIKEOUT TEAM

P	Dean Chance; Bill Hands
C	Johnny Bench (148)
1B	Dave Kingman (153)
2B	Bobby Knoop (144)
3B	Mike Schmidt (180)
SS	Woody Held (118)
LF	Dave Nicholson (175)
CF	Bobby Bonds (189)
RF	Reggie Jackson (171)
DH	Gary Alexander (166)

BENCH: Mickey Mantle; Willie Stargell; Gorman Thomas; Frank Howard; Harmon Killebrew; Dick McAuliffe; Butch Hobson

The first observation here is probably obvious: This is a terrific team. Second observation: It would be a lot of fun to watch these guys play.

Willie Stargell and Mickey Mantle are two and three on the all-time K parade (behind Reggie Jackson), but neither had individual seasons bad enough to break into our starting lineup. Some of the other team members are truly surprising. Bobby Knoop, a career .236 hitter—and an excellent fielder—hit only 56 career home runs; his strikeout total is truly terrible. Woody Held played fourteen seasons, most of them with Cleveland, which may explain the fact that he struck out 24 out of every 100 at bats, one of the worst rates in baseball history. Dave Nicholson was a bonus baby, much heralded, in the early sixties. He could hit a ball very far, but did so very seldom. Dave's 175 strikeouts were achieved in his only full major league season; who knows what he could have accomplished with more at bats? Of course with a .212 lifetime batting average it was almost impossible to convince anyone to give him that opportunity.

Nicholson was the Dave Kingman of his time—except with a better personality, which really is not saying all that much. Kingman has the highest strikeout rate in history, .297, or 30 Ks per 100 at bats! (Reggie is second at .251.)

Bobby Bonds holds the all-time single season record with his 189 whiffs in 1970, the year he batted .302, the highest average of his career. (Bobby, by the way, has a brother named Robert.)

How about a quiz? One player in major league history has struck out 100 times or more in ten consecutive seasons.

Answer: You guessed it—Reggie Jackson.

Oh yes, about Dean Chance. Dean strode forthrightly to the plate 75 times in 1965 . . . and struck out 56 times. With a good optometrist we wonder whether . . . on second thought, forget it.

And, finally, hats off to Bill Hands who struck out 14 times in a row for the Cubbies in 1968. And to Juan Eichelberger who duplicated Hands' feat in 1980 with the Padres.

THE GRACEFUL TEAM

P   Sandy Koufax; Juan Marichal; Jim Palmer;
Warren Spahn
C   Carlton Fisk
1B   Gil Hodges
2B   Jerry Coleman
3B   Brooks Robinson
SS   Mark Belanger
LF   Joe DiMaggio
CF   Willie Mays
RF   Roberto Clemente

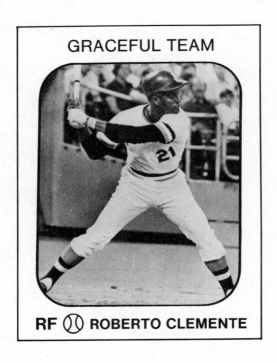

GRACEFUL TEAM

RF ⚾ ROBERTO CLEMENTE

Okay, I recognize right off the bat that this is a controversial team. My choices can be challenged at every posi-

tion. For instance, Marty Marion or the wondrous Ozzie Smith could have been chosen shortstop. Graig Nettles is a beauty at third. Satchel Paige and Ewell Blackwell were no ugly ducklings on the mound. Other selections could be made into the night. But I make no apologies for this team; each and every player here brings a smile . . . even a tingle of pleasure. The images they bring to mind are what the game of baseball is all about.

THE UNBECOMING TEAM

P   Don Mossi; Sad Sam Jones; Roger Craig;
       Fernando Valenzuela
C   Yogi Berra and Andy Etchebarren (tie)
1B   Moose Skowron
2B   Horace Clarke
3B   Felix Mantilla
SS   Honus Wagner
LF   Danny Napoleon
CF   Tommy Agee
RF   Babe Ruth
DH   Cliff Johnson
MANAGER: Harvey Kuenn
OWNER: William Wrigley, Jr.

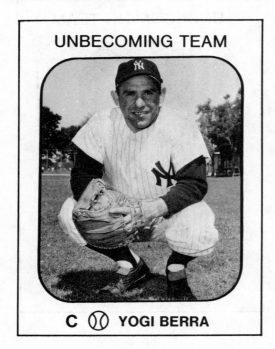

UNBECOMING TEAM

C   YOGI BERRA

A lot of people wanted me to call this team by another, somewhat more heavy-handed word. But I am good-hearted and kind and do not want to cause anyone any pain. On the other hand, have you ever seen a picture of Don Mossi? Lord, talk about the luck of the draw.

Don should be comfortable in this group as no one here will be gracing the pages of *Gentleman's Quarterly.* We hope.

Honorable mention on this team goes to Choo Choo Coleman of the early Mets. Unbelievably, he played worse than he looked.

Berra and Etchebarren finished in a dead heat for the catcher's spot. They both richly deserve such a distinction.

UNBECOMING TEAM

P ⚾ DON MOSSI

THE HANDSOME TEAM

P   Christy Mathewson; Jim Palmer; Tom Seaver
C   Carlton Fisk
1B   Steve Garvey
2B   Bobby Avila
3B   Buddy Bell
SS   Bucky Dent
LF   Jim Rice
CF   Lee Mazzilli
RF   Ken Singleton

BENCH: Rod Carew; Dick Stuart; Roberto Clemente; Bobby Richardson; King Kelly; Jimmy Piersall; Tito Francona; Mickey Mantle; Ralph Terry; Ryne Sandberg

MANAGER: Tony LaRussa

There is no handsome owner listed here because there is no such animal as a handsome owner. Cigars clenched in teeth for decades will distort even the most classically arranged features. I will, however, magnanimously give a tip of the hat to Ted Turner, who, for an owner, ain't bad.

I wonder whether Tony LaRussa and Lee Mazzilli make up for the mistake of Yogi Berra and Don Mossi? This must be what Ying & Yang means.

THE ISN'T-IT-A-SHAME-THEY-WERE-INJURED-SO-MUCH TEAM

P   Herb Score; Mark Fidrych; Karl Spooner;
        Steve Busby
C   Ray Fosse
1B   Ron Blomberg
2B   Don Zimmer
3B   Jim Ray Hart
SS   Bobby Valentine
LF   Tom Tresh
CF   Pete Reiser
RF   Tony Conigliaro
BENCH: Don Gullett; Chuck Estrada; Jimmie Hall;
        Mike Fornieles; Bobby Tolan; Larry Hisle;
        Rico Carty
CANDIDATES: Kirk Gibson; Joe Charboneau

In Ray Fosse's first full year in the major leagues, 1970, he made the American League All-Star team. In that game he was run over at the plate by Pete Rose and suffered shoulder muscle and ligament damage. He missed a month, then came back and finished the season with a .307 average, though his power seemed diminished. Less than a year later Fosse was hit by a pitch from Bill Deheny and charged the mound, where he was spiked in the hand and suffered serious tendon damage. From that point on, Fosse's power, which accounted for 18 homers in 1970, disappeared almost completely. Many sportswriters and ball players felt that after the collision with Rose, Fosse never regained his competitive edge. A potentially great career snuffed out.

Ron Blomberg had the sweetest baseball swing imaginable. Shoulder trouble ruined the muscular slugger's career—though he had a lifetime .293 average, he never played in more than 107 games in a single season.

Don Zimmer, many forget, was not born middle-aged. In fact, he was one of the brightest prospects in the Brooklyn organization, which had a plethora of talent. Then Zim was nearly killed in a 1953 beaning. He fought back after missing nearly a year, and in his first big league season hit 15 home runs in part-time duty. Then tragedy struck again when a Hal Jeffcoat pitch shattered his cheek in 1956—at the time, Zimmer was hitting .307. He missed the rest of the year and was never the same player—and who would have been?

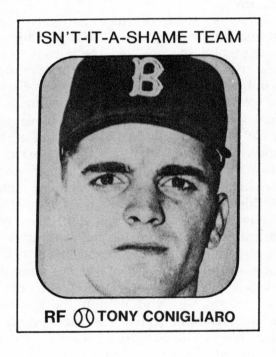

ISN'T-IT-A-SHAME TEAM

RF TONY CONIGLIARO

Jim Ray Hart averaged 28 homers with the San Francisco Giants in his first five major league seasons

(1964–68). Then, in 1969, he was beaned early in the season and later hit by a Bob Gibson fastball with such force that shoulder surgery was required. Hart played six more years, averaging only 5 homers.

Bobby Valentine broke his ankle before his career ever got going, but those who saw him before the bone-crushing accident still marvel at his skills. He managed over 200 at bats only three times in his career, often playing with an obvious limp.

After Tommy Tresh, the AL Rookie of the Year in 1962, hurt his knee his batting average fell 100 points in a matter of four years. At age thirty-one, with a .195 average, he retired.

Pete Reiser is captain of this team. Tony Conigliaro is his lieutenant. Both were certain Hall of Famers who, in only their second seasons, led their leagues in hitting and home runs respectively. Reiser's unraveling came as a result of his fearless pursuit of fly balls. He averaged 86 games a year for his ten-year career; playing as a shell of his former self he still managed a .295 lifetime average.

Tony C's story is truly horrible. During a 1967 night game, the youngest man to reach 100 home runs in baseball history was struck by a Jack Hamilton fastball, which dislocated his jaw, shattered his cheek bone, and severely damaged his eyesight. He missed the rest of 1967 and all of 1968. He amazed the baseball world by returning in 1969, despite permanent vision impairment. Incredibly, he hit 20 home runs that year and 36 in 1970. After a 1971 trade to the Angels—a move that angered Boston fans devoted to the popular native son—his eyesight began to deteriorate, and with it his spirits. He announced his retirement halfway through the season. Four years later he tried again, back with the Red Sox, but had run out of miracles, and hit .123.

Then in 1982 the world crashed in on Tony C. He suffered a massive stroke at age thirty-seven and as of this writing is in a nursing home, incapable of caring for himself. The baseball world is still rooting for you, Tony.

Herb Score's 1957 disaster may be the best documented and dramatic of all injuries. A line drive off the bat of Gil MacDougal snuffed out a wondrous young career. Score won 36 games in his first two seasons, leading the league in strikeouts both years! It is both saddening and tantalizing to contemplate what Score could have achieved in baseball.

For Larry Hisle it is already too late. For Kirk Gibson and Joe Charboneau, powerful but fragile young men, it may be the beginning of the end.

It is also the end for the loveable, colorful Mark "The Bird" Fidrych, who, at age 29, rather than be released outright, retired from the Red Sox's Triple A Pawtucket team. You'll be missed Mark—and remembered for the joy you brought to the game of baseball.

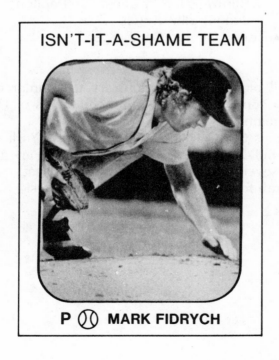

ISN'T-IT-A-SHAME TEAM

P MARK FIDRYCH

THE NEW YORK CITY TEAM

P   Sandy Koufax; Whitey Ford; Dennis Leonard; Johnny Murphy
C   Joe Torre
1B   Lou Gehrig
2B   Frankie Frisch
3B   Sid Gordon
SS   Phil Rizzuto
LF   Hank Greenberg
CF   Tommy Davis
RF   Richie Zisk

BENCH: Rod Carew; Terry Crowley; Lee Mazzilli; Ed Kranepool; Lou Whitaker; Julio Cruz; John Candelaria; Willie Randolph; Frank Torre; Frank Malzone; Snuffy Stirnweiss; Billy Loes; Joe Pepitone; Joe Judge; Billy Jurges

MANAGER: George Bamberger

Baseball players do not, contrary to popular delusion, have to come exclusively from the states of California and Alabama.

Perhaps Sid Gordon typifies the New York City ball player. Sid died playing softball in Central Park at the age of fifty-seven—still doing what he loved best.

Hurrah for the Big Apple! Go youse guys!

THE FIZZLE TEAM

(Fizzle: to fail, especially after a successful beginning.)

P	Bob Grim; Don Schwall; Rawley Eastwick; Boo Ferriss
C	Earl Williams
1B	Curt Blefary
2B	Elio Chacon
3B	Ted Cox
SS	Phil Linz
LF	Steve Henderson
CF	Rich Coggins
RF	Danny Walton

BENCH: Bill Stafford; Harry Byrd; Clint Hurdle
MANAGER: John McNamara

This team is made up of players who started their careers off with a bang—fielding, hitting, and throwing with such skill and effectiveness that their names were on the lips of thousands of fans across the country.

Then, poof. *Le deluge.* (Without major injury being the cause.)

Examples: Bob Grim, Rookie of the Year in the American League in 1954 when he won 20 games, won 40 games the rest of his career. Boo Ferriss had 21 wins in his rookie year, 1945, and 25 wins in 1946. Then he won only 19 games in the next four years with ERAs of 4.04, 5.23, 4.05, and 18.00! That's all folks.

Phil Linz, another Yankee, hit .287 his rookie year, then dropped to .269 and .250, before the bottom fell completely out: .207, .200, .222, .207, .209. Good grief. Phil gave up baseball ostensibly to play the harmonica full time. (For the uninitiated, in 1964 Linz pulled out a harmonica and played "Mary Had a Little Lamb" on the Yankee bus after the team's fourth straight loss to the

47

White Sox, infuriating rookie manager Yogi Berra and nearly causing a fistfight. Linz got the last laugh: he was fined $200 by Berra—and weeks later signed a $20,000 promotional contract with the Horner Harmonica Company.)

Rich Coggins hit .333 and .319 his first two years in the majors. The next three years he hit .243, .236, and .160. Then mercifully, it was over.

Ted Cox got hits his first 6 times up in the major leagues. Even the long-suffering Red Sox fans became optimistic about Ted. They shouldn't have. (Lifetime batting average: .245.)

Don Schwall and Curt Blefary were Rookies of the Year too. Blefary's lifetime batting average was .237. The year after his rookie season Schwall's ERA went from 3.22 to 4.94! Boston traded him immediately. Good move.

Earl Williams hit 33 homers his first season and was the National League's Rookie of the Year. He hung on for a total of eight years, gaining weight, striking out, and hitting .247.

In Danny Walton's first full season he slammed 17 homers in only 117 games. He hit a total of 11 more in his career.

Steve Henderson, the man traded for Tom Seaver, was a reserve outfielder on the 1981 Cubs. Enough said.

McNamara had the best record in the majors managing the Reds in 1981. He didn't make it halfway through 1982.

Oddest Fizzle Department: Brooklyn Dodgers pitcher Dan Bankhead hit a home run on the first pitch of his first major league at bat. He never hit another.

THE AMOROUS TEAM

P	Darcy Fast; Peter Loos
C	Conrad Darling
1B	Pete LaCock
2B	Jacob Virtue
3B	Michael Hickey
SS	Johnny Clapp
LF	Thomas Letcher
CF	Virgin Cannell
RF	Seymour Studley
BENCH:	Edward Hug; Ernest Koy; Rodney Graber; Paul Casanova; Ellis Valentine; Rick Sweet; Sandy Amoros; Charles Manlove

Some of the names on this team I am simply not going to comment on; this is a family book.

However, if Charlie Manlove volunteers to coach Junior's little league team I recommend you keep your eyes wide open.

We also can't help but wonder whether any of these fellows married. Can you imagine Harriet Hickey or Sally Studley? Darlene Darling? Louise Loos? Clara Clapp? Okay, I'll stop.

THE INTOXICANT NAME TEAM

(Warning to parents: *Keep this page from your teenage sons and daughters.*)

P	Frank Reisling; Larry Sherry; David Vineyard; Herbert Hash
C	Norm Sherry
1B	Herman Schaefer
2B	Jerry Remy
3B	Melvin Roach
SS	Bobby Wine
LF	Tinsley Ginn
CF	Eugene Rye
RF	William Hemp
BENCH:	John Boozer; Robert Rush; Randy Lerch; William Lush; Andy High; Jim Coker

I love Tinsley Ginn's name. And Eugene Rye's nickname was "Half Pint," which I also like.

All of these guys are probably mighty sick of word plays and other clever jokes about their god-given names. I, however, don't care how they feel. With a name like Frank Downs Coffey (And how many names do you know that are complete sentences?), it's about time I got some revenge.

THE ROBINSON TEAM

(Best year in parenthesis)

P   Don Robinson (14–6);
       Hank Robinson (12–7)
C   Wilbert Robinson (.353; 1 HR; 98 RBIs)
1B   Eddie Robinson (.296; 22 HRs; 104 RBIs)
2B   Jackie Robinson (.342; 16 HRs; 124 RBIs)
3B   Brooks Robinson (.317; 28 HRs; 118 RBIs)
SS   Craig Robinson (.230; 0 HRs; 29 RBIs)
LF   Floyd Robinson (.312; 11 HRs; 109 RBIs)
CF   Bill Robinson (.304; 26 HRs; 104 RBIs)
RF   Frank Robinson (.342; 39 HRs; 134 RBIs)
MANAGER: Uncle Robby Robinson

For purposes of having a Robinson manager, Wilbert Robinson the player became Uncle Robby Robinson the manager. I hope no one objects. Uncle Robby certainly wouldn't—his disposition was among the sunniest the game has ever seen. Plus, he was an excellent manager, winning pennants with Brooklyn in 1916 and 1920.

Who was the best Robinson? A tough call, but the nod goes to Frank, the only player in baseball history to be MVP of both the National and American Leagues.

Craig wasn't much of a shortstop but played six years, and every team has to have a shortstop. Craig's it.

But the rest of this team is very good indeed.

Quite a family. Mom and Dad should be proud.

THE DON'T-BELIEVE-THESE-GUYS-FOR-A-MINUTE TEAM

P	William Malarkey; Eugene Krapp; John Poser
C	Terry Bulling
1B	James Outlaw
2B	Bert Conn
3B	Ray Barker
SS	Tom Lawless
LF	Earl Rapp
CF	Bill Sharp
RF	Freddy Leach
OWNER:	Ray Kroc
HONORARY MEMBERS:	Reggie Jackson; Billy Martin; George Steinbrenner

Silly? You bet. But if Freddy Leach promises you he's finally going to leave next week, don't believe him for a minute.

Eugene Krapp's nickname was "Rubber Arm." He pitched for four years. Well, not that rubbery.

THE WORST-FIELDING TEAM

P   Sparky Lyle
C   Dick Dietz
1B   Dick Stuart
2B   George Grantham
3B   Richie Allen
SS   Don Buddin
LF   Lou Novikoff
CF   Jim Hickman
RF   Reggie Jackson
BENCH: Marv Throneberry; Dave Kingman; Joe
       Foy; Alex Johnson; Sonny Jackson; Fer-
       ris Fain; Jesse Gonder

To quote Met pitcher Roger Craig after a season in which he lost 24 games, "You have to be pretty good to lose so many games." Similarly, to commit lots of errors you have to be doing something pretty well. Usually it's hitting, though Met centerfielder Jim Hickman (1962–64) is an example of a guy who neither fielded nor hit.

Sparky Lyle might be a surprise selection as worst-fielding pitcher, but anyone who has seen old Spark plod off the mound, mechanically pick up a bunt, and throw an uncatchable slider to various bases, will know what we're talking about.

In 1970, Dick Deitz had an amazing 25 passed balls to go with his 14 errors. He hit .300, which didn't nearly balance the ledger.

Dick Stuart, appropriately nicknamed "Dr. Strange-glove," holds the major league record for most years leading the league in errors (seven between 1958–64). In 1961 he managed 21 errors and in 1963 a horrid 29. Various managers tried to explain to Dick that if he didn't catch the ball at first base the umpire would consistently call the runner safe. Dick never seemed to care.

"Marvelous" Marv Throneberry was a close second at first.

George Grantham's nickname was "Boots." In 1924 he committed 55 errors, then turned it around in 1925 and had only 44. Boots is probably the worst fielder ever to play baseball.

Richie Allen, the awesome power hitter of the sixties and seventies, made 41 errors in 1964, 26 in 1965, and 35 in 1967, all for the obviously patient Phillies. Richie cared slightly more than Dick Stuart; they played in the same Phillie infield in 1965. Now that must have been something to see.

When Don Buddin got it going with the Red Sox in 1956 he managed consecutive seasons of 29, 31, 35, 30, and 23 errors before management wised up and traded him far away. The standard Beantown joke went like this: Why is Don Buddin like the Ancient Mariner? He stoppeth one of three.

Lou Novikoff, who led three minor leagues in hitting, was once instructed by manager Charlie Grimm: "There are two ways for you to field a ball. Lie down in front of it, or simply wait until the ball stops rolling. In either case, when it has safely stopped moving, pick the ball up and throw it toward third so we can hold the batter to a double." Lou was released after a season in which he hit .304—you know how bad he had to have been.

Enough about Jim Hickman. If God had given him more physical ability he would have done a lot better.

Reggie Jackson holds the American League record for most years (five) leading outfielders in errors (1968–70, '72, '75, '76). The amazing thing about Reggie is that he staunchly defends himself as an outfielder, which is absurd. In recent years he has cut down on his errors by employing Charlie Grimm's dictum of waiting until the ball has stopped, or when Reg is feeling particularly confident, of picking it up right before it stops. Few outfielders have ever been worse at charging the ball in right field. Reggie isn't very good at going back on the ball either.

Honorable Mention: Ferris Fain led the Pacific Coast League in errors four times, and the American League five times. A consistent player.

Odd Random Fact Department: Ty Cobb, a good out-fielder, committed the most errors of any player in major league history. (He played in 3,033 games over twenty-four years.)

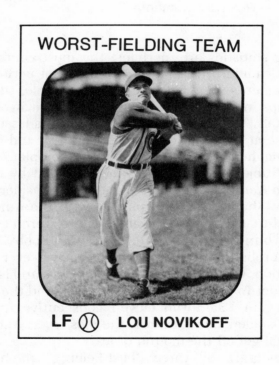

WORST-FIELDING TEAM

LF LOU NOVIKOFF

THE BEST-FIELDING TEAM

P   Bobby Shantz; Warren Spahn; Jim Kaat
C   Johnny Bench
1B   Wes Parker
2B   Nellie Fox
3B   Brooks Robinson
SS   Luis Aparicio
LF   Carl Yastrzemski
CF   Curt Flood
RF   Roberto Clemente

Fielding statistics are, perhaps, the most controversial and misleading of all the major statistical performance measurements. Year after year, for example, the finest shortstops in either league will also have relatively high error totals. Why? Because they get to balls lesser lights just wave at. Number of chances handled, and chances per game help here, but aren't the complete answer either. Subjective fielding awards, decided by the *The Sporting News* among others, were also considered.

Bobby Shantz, the tiny pitcher with the quick feet, won eight Golden Glove awards. There weren't a lot of sacrifice bunts performed successfully on Bobby. Warren Spahn, probably the most complete player ever to play his position, was also superb with the glove and is the all-time leader in double plays by a pitcher. And the ageless wonder, Jim Kaat, won eleven consecutive American League Golden Glove awards, the most ever. And at age 44 he still got off the mound quickly.

Interestingly, all three "best-fielding" pitchers are left-handed.

Johnny Bench was *The Sporting News'* best-fielding catcher for ten consecutive years (1968–77). Injuries in recent years have made many forget what a truly great arm Bench had behind the plate. There have been so many great catchers through the years (including Yogi Berra, Roy Campanella, Elston Howard, Mickey Cochrane, Bill Dickey, Johnny Edwards, Bill Freehan, and today Jim Sundberg and Gary Carter) that Bench's choice may have been the toughest selection of The Best-Fielding Team.

Wes Parker, the slick left-handed first baseman of the slick-fielding Dodger teams of the sixties, led the National League in fielding for six consecutive years (1967–72), and committed a total of only 45 errors in his brief nine-year career. His fielding average of .996 is the highest ever. The Brewers' Cecil Cooper and the Mets' Keith Hernandez are probably the current best at first. Other greats include Gil Hodges, Frank McCormick, Vic Power, George Scott, and Eddie Waitkus.

Nellie Fox did not have the greatest range but in the crucial measurement of total chances per game, Fox was first in the American League six times and second five times. He led the league in double plays five times. He's tied for the highest all-time fielding average (.984), is third in putouts, fifth in assists, fourth in chances, and second in double plays. Fox's long time manager Al Lopez said it best: "Nellie Fox hustled his way to stardom."

Second base is another position that has seen a great many superb gloves, including Bill Mazeroski, Bobby Doerr, Bobby Knoop, Jerry Adair, Eddie Collins, Charlie Gehringer, Billy Herman, Jerry Priddy (one of those fellows who just seems to have been forgotten, a great glove for eleven American League seasons, primarily in the late forties and fifties), and Red Schoendienst. Today's best is probably Manny Trillo, with plenty of competition from Kansas City's Frank White and Baltimore's Rich Dauer. Bobby Grich was, at one time, a terrific second baseman but a serious back injury ruined his range and flexibililty.

There is little doubt that Brooks Robinson is the greatest-fielding third baseman in baseball history. It is ironic that the second-best–fielding third baseman, Graig Nettles, was forced to play at the height of his own career in Robinson's large shadow. Today's best is Buddy Bell as Nettles, who will be thirty-nine in 1983, has begun to slow down. The Phillies' Mike Schmidt is also excellent.

Great shortstops may be the most enjoyable of all players to watch since they must be both quick and fast, acrobatic, spontaneous, and possess great versatility. The best-fielding shortstop was another absurdly difficult decision. Luis Aparicio, the lightning quick, strong-armed mainstay of the excellent White Sox teams of the fifties and sixties (Luis also played with Baltimore and Boston) leads all shortstops in assists and double plays, is third in chances, sixth in putouts, and seventh in fielding percentage. He led AL shortstops in fielding eight consecutive years. Ah, but the competition is wondrous too. Mark Belanger has the highest fielding average ever in the American League. Pee Wee Reese and Phil Rizzuto were both superb (and should be in the Hall), Eddie Brinkman, Roy McMillan, Lou Boudreau, Dal Maxvil, and Dick Groat all had excellent gloves. Today's fans can enjoy Robin Yount, Ozzie Smith, and, hopefully, Rick Burleson, should he be able to complete a comeback from rotator cuff problems. Dave Concepcion, now slowing down a bit, has been very good for ten years, perhaps a bit more spectacular than he is consistent.

Left fielders are usually the outfield's weak sisters, stuck out there so they don't have to throw too far, told to play deep so the shortstop can run out and catch pop-ups, and generally expected to keep a low profile until they get up to bat. Carl Yastrzemski was an exception. He led the AL in fielding seven times and led or tied in assists five times. Yaz had a strong and very accurate throwing arm, played Fenway's "Green Monster" as though he designed it, and got a great jump on the ball. Today's best is probably Dave Winfield, who is fast, tall enough to jump higher than outfield walls, and has a rifle arm. Oakland's Rickey Henderson is good and getting better.

Curt Flood is the author's choice for center field in another impossibly close race. Flood once handled 568 consecutive chances without making an error, which is the major league record. He could run, throw, go back on the ball. In short, he could do it all. But, again, the competition gives one pause: Jimmy Piersall and Dom DiMaggio, Max Carey, Tris Speaker, Willie Mays, Jim Landis, Paul Blair, and Richie Ashburn. Whew.

Today's best is probably Andre Dawson of the Expos, with Dale Murphy and John Shelby not far behind. Fred Lynn, before injuries started his fragile body in decline, was as graceful and daring a center fielder as the American League had seen since Paul Blair in his prime years.

Roberto Clemente is the best right fielder in the game's history. Period. Others whose memory brings a smile include the classy Al Kaline, Bobby Bonds in his heyday, Carl Furillo, and Roger Maris. Today's best is a toss-up between Boston's Dwight Evans and Tony Armas, with the Cardinals' George Hendrick and the Giants' Jack Clark close behind. What do you do when you have the game's two best right fielders? Move one of them to center.

THE LIKED-BY-ALMOST-EVERYBODY TEAM

P	Ron Guidry; Tug McGraw; Jim Kaat
C	Roy Campanella
1B	Willie Stargell
2B	Rich Dauer
3B	Sal Bando
SS	Ernie Banks
LF	Monte Irvin
CF	Minnie Minoso
RF	Stan Musial
MANAGER:	George Bamberger; Al Lopez
BENCH:	Joe Torre; Tim McCarver; Roy White; Al Kaline; Bill White; Phil Rizzuto; Charlie Grimm; Cecil Cooper; Aurelio Rodriguez; Roy Smalley

In recent years it seems like most ball players expect to be paid to sneeze in public, though this is, of course, not an altogether modern development. But the massive media attention athletes receive today, not to mention the massive dollars, has exacerbated the problem. The above fellows, and many, many more, are delightful exceptions to this regrettable rule, and we salute them. Thanks guys, your attitude's making the world a better place.

THE PEACH FUZZ TEAM

P   Joe Nuxhall (fifteen)
       David Clyde (eighteen)
       Larry Dierker (eighteen)
C   Jimmie Foxx (fifteen)
1B   Eddie Murray (twenty-one)
2B   Nellie Fox (seventeen)
3B   Eddie Mathews (twenty)
SS   Robbin Yount (eighteen)
LF   Mel Ott (sixteen)
CF   Whitey Lockman (eighteen)
RF   Tony Conigliaro (nineteen)
BENCH: Al Kaline (nineteen); Jose Oquendo (nineteen); Willie Mays (twenty); Tim Raines (twenty-one); Ed Kranepool (eighteen); Mickey Mantle (nineteen); Fernando Valenzuela (nineteen)
MANAGER: Joe Cronin (twenty-six)

Joe Nuxhall is the youngest man to ever play in a major league game. At fifteen he pitched two-thirds of an inning, walked 5, gave up 2 hits, and had an ERA of 67.50. The Reds sent him down for "seasoning," clearly a good move, and didn't recall him for eight years. David Clyde was 4–8 as an eighteen year old with the Texas Rangers. He pitched parts of three other seasons in the majors and when last heard from was still trying. Larry Dierker pitched and won his first big league game on his eighteenth birthday in 1964.

Jimmie Foxx played in 76 minor league games at age fifteen and hit .296. At sixteen he was on the Tigers' bench and at seventeen hit .313.

Eddie Murray had 27 homers, 88 RBIs, and a .283 average as the American League's Rookie of the Year in 1977. They should have brought him up sooner.

Nellie Fox hit .325 and .304 with two minor league teams as a sixteen year old. At seventeen, in 1945, he led his minor league in hits, runs, at bats, and was the All-Star second baseman. Military service got in the way and Nellie wasn't a big-league regular until twenty-two. He played nineteen excellent years.

Robin Yount was a full-timer at eighteen for the Brewers, batting .250, and has gotten better and better and better. The AL 1982 MVP was a nine-year veteran at age twenty-eight.

Eddie Mathews was a regular with the Boston Braves at age twenty in 1952. He hit 25 home runs, and it was all downhill for major league pitchers for the next seventeen years.

Mel Ott made the New York Giants at sixteen and hit .383 at seventeen in limited duty. As a full-time regular at nineteen he hit .322 with 18 homers. Another Giant, Whitey Lockman, was equally precocious, hitting .341 at age eighteen.

Tony Conigliaro waited until nineteen to reach the Red Sox and then knocked 24 home runs. Tony got a close nod over Willie Mays, who at twenty hit .274 with 20 homers, and Al Kaline, who at twenty hit .340, to become the youngest man ever to win the batting title.

Joe Cronin won the 1933 pennant as the twenty-six-year-old manager of the Washington Senators. He also hit .309.

At age eighteen Ed Kranepool played three games for the terrible 1962 Mets; it aged him considerably.

THE DISLIKED-BY-NEARLY-EVERYONE TEAM

P	Jim Coates; Mike Marshall; Jim Bouton
C	Clint Courtney
1B	Dave Kingman
2B	Rogers Hornsby
3B	John McGraw
SS	Leo Durocher
LF	Alex Johnson
CF	Ty Cobb
RF	Reggie Jackson
MANAGER:	Dick Williams

Jim Coates, a rattlesnake-mean Southerner who pitched for the Yankees in the fifties and sixties, threw constantly at the heads of opposing hitters, despite admonitions from his own teammates to cut it out. Mike Marshall, an intelligent man, got along with almost no one—except Jim Bouton. Maybe that says it all.

Clint Courtney was described by Satchel Paige, when they were teammates, as "the meanest man I ever met."

At the beginning of Dave Kingman's career he was an enigma; many simply couldn't figure him out. Now, years later, ball players and press agree there's no reason to try and figure him out. He refuses to try to improve either his fielding or his strikeout ratio, wants nothing to do with his teammates, and acts like the world owes him something. It does: a swift kick in the butt.

Rogers Hornsby was the Dave Kingman of his time—he had nothing good to say about anyone. The feeling was mutual.

John McGraw, the Hall of Fame manager, was perhaps the most hated ball player in history, with the possible exception of Ty Cobb. Nothing was beneath McGraw, including tripping runners as they rounded third base. He fought with umpires, teammates, opponents, sportswriters, league presidents, and old friends—a dreadfully unhappy and altogether unpleasant fellow.

Leo Durocher is the type of guy whose press clippings make him sound colorful, rather than obnoxious (which is far more accurate). His "nice guys finish last" says it all. Leo's monstrous ego made playing with him or for him an impossible task.

Alex Johnson's teammate on the California Angels, Chico Ruiz, once said on hearing Johnson complain about whites disliking him: "I'm as black as you are . . . and I don't dislike you, I hate you." Practically everyone agreed.

Ty Cobb was described by fellow Hall of Famer Hugh Jennings as "loathsome," a just tribute to a man whose tactics both on and off the field were universally deplored.

Reggie Jackson is another guy whose press clippings don't tell the story. Reggie comes off as bright, articulate, and even modest on television. In reality his ego knows no bounds; if Jackson is not in complete control of a situation he is unhappy, often paranoid. Complex. Fragile. Utterly self-centered.

THE BICEP TEAM

P	J.R. Richard; Nolan Ryan
C	Lance Parrish
1B	Ted Kluszewski
2B	Bobby Grich
3B	Harmon Killebrew
SS	Honus Wagner
LF	Hack Wilson
CF	Mickey Mantle
RF	Reggie Jackson

BENCH: Luke Easter; Frank Howard; Boog Powell; Willie McCovey; Jimmie Foxx; Jim Rice; Don Baylor; Brian Downing

We're talking muscles here, not necessarily height or girth, or even the ability to use the muscles you have; just sheer bicep bulk. And, again, we're into a very subjective area, with yours truly the ultimate judge and jury.

J.R. Richard is a choice I don't think many will find fault with. Pitchers are very often extremely large fellows, larger than the average fan supposes. Nolan Ryan, for example, seems trim but not bulky when seen on television or even from a box seat. In person he's very muscular in appearance; he's actually a dedicated weight lifter who looks like he could crush one's head like a grape. Nolan's real first name is Lyn, but he doesn't like it and I urge you not to use it unless fool-proof shelter is nearby.

Lance Parrish didn't used to be huge, then he began to pump iron for real (often with the Angels' Brian Downing, another brute), and now can barely fit into his uniform. Lance's manager, Sparky Anderson, violently opposed his catcher's weight training during the season. Sparky is also five-nine with few perceptible remaining muscles. Lance kept pumping, and was the AL's starting All-Star catcher in 1982. Sparkey shut up—a rare occurrence.

Big Klu used to cut the sleeves of his short-sleeved Cincinnati Reds uniform practically up to the shoulder, exposing acres of bicep. Impressed the hell out of me, scared opposing pitchers, and made him the least-likely-butt-of-a-practical joke in major league history.

BICEP TEAM

1B TED KLUSZEWSKI

Bobby Grich has the biggest muscles of the legions of wimpy second basemen who have played baseball.

Honus Wagner was strong and bulky, his build a thoroughly atypical body type for a shortstop. No other man who ever played shortstop weighed over 150 pounds.

Harmon Killebrew and Hack Wilson, at third and left,

were both relatively short, and enormously muscular. Neither were sculpted in any way, their bodies bulging out at every possible location.

Mickey Mantle and Reggie Jackson are another pair of book ends. Both are startlingly short, five-ten and five-eleven, and look remarkably powerful, particularly in the upper body. It takes only one quick glance to see why both were the tape-measure home run kings of their respective eras.

I was tempted to make some sort of clever, snide remark to finish off this section but upon reflection thought better of it. There is often a correlation between temper and musculature—at least there was at my high school—and I'm not taking any chances.

The author weighs 145 pounds and would not receive consideration for anyone's all-bicep team.

BICEP TEAM

3B HARMON KILLEBREW

THE SWITCH-HITTING TEAM

P   Early Wynn; Jerry Walker
C   Ted Simmons
1B   Eddie Murray
2B   Jim Gilliam
3B   Pete Rose
SS   Garry Templeton
LF   Reggie Smith
CF   Mickey Mantle
RF   Ken Singleton
BENCH: Willie Wilson; Maury Wills; Willie McGee; Tim Raines; Roy Smalley; Lee Mazzilli; George Wright

Early Wynn, who won 300 games in twenty-three years of pitching, batted right-handed for the first five years of his career, then "switched" to switching in 1945 and promptly batted .319. He ended up at a respectable .214, including 17 homers and 173 RBIs. Jerry Walker, primarily an American Leaguer in the fifties and sixties, took the opposite route, leaving switch-hitting the last two years of his career. And it's hard to figure why. The last three years he batted both ways, Jerry hit .368, .250, and .263. In 1963, after being traded to Cleveland, he hit right-handed at a .105 clip. And he stayed with it in 1964 and managed a .000. Once a switcher, always a switcher. You can't go back in life, Jerry.

Ted Simmons, a lifetime .293 hitter, is the best switch-hitting catcher in history. No contest. Plus he's a nice guy.

Eddie Murray, the 1977 American League Rookie of the Year, could catch Mantle to become the greatest switch-hitter of them all. In six years he's never hit less than 22 homers and he's only twenty-seven years old. And he's a superb fielder.

68

Jim Gilliam was a great table setter for the excellent Dodger teams of the fifties and sixties. Always near the top in walks, he was a lifetime .265 batter and one of the league's finest fielders. Jim died at the age of fifty, two days before he was to take the coaching lines for the Dodgers against the Yankees in the 1978 World Series. We remember you, Junior.

Why aren't there more switch-hitting third basemen? One theory has it that anyone dumb enough to position themselves so close to the batters is also too dumb to learn how to switch-hit. Pete Rose isn't dumb; and with a bat in his hand he's a genius. "Charlie Hustle" hasn't played third since 1979. The author hopes no one objects to his selection.

Garry Templeton is a career .300 hitter who became in 1979 the first man in history to collect 100 or more hits from both sides of the plate in a single season. (The marvelous Willie Wilson duplicated the feat in 1980.) To do it, Garry batted right-handed exclusively for the last two weeks of the season.

Reggie Smith, from both sides of the plate, has one of the most powerful and picturesque batting swings ever seen. He's over 300 career home runs and holds the National League record for most home runs by a switcher in two consecutive seasons (61, in 1977–78).

Mickey Mantle, as far as this fan is concerned, is *the* switch hitter of all time. Granted, this isn't exactly a controversial stand. But as an adult who once spent countless hours emulating Mantle's stance in front of the mirror, I felt it needed to be stated. For the record. (Mick, by the way, hit home runs from both sides of the plate in a single game ten times in his career—a record.) The mind's eye treasures the memory of Mantle's awesome swing. Thanks, Mick.

For other New York fans, Ken Singleton's name instantly brings to mind early Met trading blunders. A native New Yorker, Kenny was foolishly let go. A career

.290 hitter, he's still producing as he gracefully enters his twilight years with the fortunate Baltimore Orioles.

Idle Thought Department: Hank Aguirre, the terrible-hitting pitcher (.085 lifetime), tried switch-hitting between 1965 and 1968 and hit .086, .120, .500 (1 for 2, let's not get excited here), and .000. In 1969 he went back to his natural right-handed stance and stunned the baseball world by hitting .400 (2 for 5). How to frighten 'em, big guy!

Idle Fact Department: The 1976 Cardinals had seven switch hitters on their roster, the most ever (Kessinger, Simmons, R. Smith, Templeton, Mumphrey, Harris, and Tamargo).

THE COURAGE TEAM

P   Lou Brissie; John Hiller; Blue Moon Odom
C   Roy Campanella
1B   Lou Gehrig
2B   Ron Hunt
3B   Jackie Robinson
SS   Don Zimmer
LF   Bob Cerv
CF   Pete Reiser
RF   Pete Gray
HONORABLE MENTION: Andre Thornton; Tony Conigliaro; Tony Oliva; Ted Williams; Ralph Houk; J.R. Richard
MANAGER: Harvey Kuenn

There are so many kinds of courage and so many degrees of it that we wanted to make it clear from the start that the courage Jackie Robinson showed is so different from say, the wartime courage of Ralph Houk, that to compare one to the other runs the risk of diminishing both.

Courage comes in different forms at different times. This is a team to admire, for a variety of reasons; whether one form of courage is greater or lesser than another I don't pretend to know. What I do know is that all these men are worthy of our respect.

Lou Brissie's story is truly an amazing one. Brissie was badly wounded in action in World War II. A portion of one leg was lost, the other was badly mangled. (Brissie was the only survivor in a patrol of twelve men.) He had twenty-three operations in the next two years, had a partial artificial leg attached, and began to play ball again. Incredibly, in 1947 he won 23 games in the minor leagues and the next year the Philadelphia Athletics brought him up. Lou won 14 games in 1948. Sixteen in 1949. He retired in 1953 at age twenty-nine with a major league record of 44–48—and the respect of baseball fans and players everywhere.

John Hiller came back from a serious heart attack to pitch for the Detroit Tigers for seven years. The attack occurred in January of 1971 after Hiller had been a big league pitcher for four seasons. He was twenty-seven years old at the time. After numerous operations, one of which resulted in the loss of a major part of his lower intestine, Hiller arrived back in the major leagues in July 1972. And in 1973 he had 38 saves to lead the major leagues. After his heart attack Hiller was actually a much better pitcher, ending up with an 82–69 record, 116 saves, and an ERA of 2.63.

Blue Moon Odom, while attempting to break up a burglary attempt during January 1972, was shot twice, in the neck and side. In the hospital Odom said that he thought he'd had all the bad luck he would ever have— and he was right. In 1971 Odom was 10–12 with a 4.71 ERA. In 1972 he was 15–6 with a 2.51 ERA and won the final American League playoff game to clinch the pennant for the Oakland A's. In the World Series, though he didn't win a game, Odom had a 1.59 ERA, contributing to the A's victory.

Blue Moon—you deserved it.

On January 28, 1958, a terrible automobile accident broke Roy Campanella's neck, nearly severing his spinal cord—and left him paralyzed for life. Anyone who has met Campy, or heard him speak, realizes what true courage is all about. Despite everything, Campy still has a joy and zest for life that characterized his attitude and play before that fateful night.

Lou Gehrig at first base. Who else?

Don Zimmer was nearly killed by a pitched ball while playing with St. Paul in the American Association in 1953. One of the brightest lights in the talent-rich Dodger organization, Zimmer was batting .300 at the time, with 23 homers and 63 RBIs in only 81 games! He came back the next year and performed well, but he wasn't the same. Then in 1956, a fastball thrown by the Reds' Hal Jeffcoat crashed into Zimmer, breaking his jaw, ending his season again. But Zimmer came back and played ten more years, bouncing most of the time between the minors and majors. Zimmer would have been a great player, almost all the experts agree. A figure of some amusement in today's button-down, Madison Avenue baseball era, Don Zimmer's reputation for real courage has not been rightly recognized. We remember, Zip.

Jackie Robinson and courage are synonymous in the minds of millions of Americans. We can still see him dancing down the basepaths, back and forth, feinting and darting, waiting for that exact moment when he would explode into the next base as though he "deserved" to be there. And, the way he played, he did.

In 1958 Bob Cerv played two months with a broken jaw that was wired shut. Confined to a liquid diet, and unable to speak a word, Cerv continued the best year of his career, ending up with 38 home runs, a .305 batting average, and 104 RBIs—for a seventh-place club, the Kansas City A's.

Pete Reiser smashed into outfield fences with such regularity that he literally ruined his own career. After his last awful collision, in 1948 at the age of thirty, he never played more than 84 games in any season again. Reiser played full tilt, all the time, and just couldn't control himself. Today he might be branded foolish; thirty years ago he was the standard of determination for the entire National League.

Pete Gray played only one season in the major leagues, during the talent-bare war year of 1945. He hit only .218 without a home run. Pete Gray had one arm.

Our bench includes war heroes (Williams and Houk), seriously injured players who played with pain (Oliva, Conigliaro, and Richard), and one man (Thornton) who has lost most of his family (wife, daughter, father) to tragedy in the last three years.

THE GOOD-MANAGERS-WHO-WERE-LOUSY-BALLPLAYERS TEAM

P	Tommy LaSorda (6.48 ERA)
	George Bamberger (9.42 ERA)
C	Ralph Houk (.272)
1B	Walt Alston (.000)
2B	Sparky Anderson (.218)
3B	Tony LaRussa (.199)
SS	Gene Mauch (.239)
LF	Whitey Herzog (.257)
CF	Dick Williams (.260)
RF	Joe Altobelli (.210)

BENCH: Possibilities here are nearly endless. There's no reason to be cruel.

Some of these statistics are deceiving, making our managerial wizards appear better than they really were. Herzog, for example, wasn't much of a fielder, played on awful teams like the Washington Senators and Kansas City Athletics, and averaged 3 home runs a year. His .257 batting average may have been God's way of saying, "There, there Dorrel Norman Elvert."

Sparky Anderson was given one year to strut his stuff. He played on the 1959 Phillie team that was dead last in the National League with a 64–90 record and hit .218. Sparky's phone never rang again.

Walter Alston appeared in one game, strode forthrightly to the plate, struck out, and never played again.

Gene Mauch was thoroughly mediocre in the field and at the plate. In nine years he hit 5 home runs. While playing and managing with Minneapolis in 1958, he was so disgusted with his own playing performance that after a game he literally nailed his spikes to the clubhouse wall. He never played another game.

A .272 average for Ralph Houk! Not bad, right? Wrong. Ralph played eight years and had a total of 158 at bats—less than 20 a year. Casey Stengel once said that "you can see a lot by observing." Old Ralph did a lot of observing.

Pitchers Tommy LaSorda and George Bamberger *together* appeared in 36 games in six years. Neither ever won a game.

Do as I say, not as I did.

THE WALKING TEAM

P   George Uhle (98)
        Red Ruffing (97)
C   Mickey Cochrane (857)
1B   Lou Gehrig (1,508)
2B   Joe Morgan (1,800)
3B   Eddie Yost (1,614)
SS   Pee Wee Reese (1,210)
LF   Ted Williams (2,019)
CF   Mickey Mantle (1,734)
RF   Babe Ruth (2,056)
BENCH: Carl Yastrzemski; Stan Musial; Mel Ott;
       Harmon Killebrew; Willie Mays

Criteria taken into consideration for The Walking Team include total walks, walking average (walks per at bat), and single-season highs.

Now the reason so many sluggers walk is probably obvious: pitchers tend to be mighty careful when a Ruth, Williams, or Mantle comes marching up to the plate.

But how can the pitchers of the American League look themselves in the eye when they together walked Eddie Yost, a .231 hitter, 151 times during the 1956 season? I would have lobbed it underhand and shamed Eddie into swinging.

The top single-season walking record, plus the top lifetime total, is held by Ruth—170 walks in 1923. Ted Williams, generally regarded as having the best eye in major league history, owns the next three best single-season walking marks (162 twice, 1947 and 1949, and 156 in 1946) and the highest walking average of all time—.208. Then comes our friend Eddie Yost. Incidently, Williams and Ruth are first and second respectively (.483 and .474) in lifetime on-base percentage.

Joe Morgan walked more times than anyone else in

National League history. Eddie Joost, a .239 lifetime hitter (1936–55) and another one of those players whom history seems to have forgotten, walked 149 times in 1949, which has a nice symmetry to it.

Catchers don't walk much. There isn't one catcher in the top fifty-five all-time walkers. Even a slugger of Johnny Bench's magnitude has only walked 867 times in his fifteen full-time big league seasons, an average of only 58 walks a year. Mickey Cochrane is at least in the top thirty-five in walking rate with .142. You'd think that catchers, seeing up close how often batters swing at pitches out of the strike zone, would be more patient themselves. But then, life is rarely logical.

THE R.B.I. TEAM

P   Red Ruffing (273)
C   Yogi Berra (1,430)
1B Lou Gehrig (1,991)
2B Rogers Hornsby (1,596)
3B Eddie Mathews (1,453)
SS Honus Wagner (1,732)
LF Ted Williams (1,839)
CF Joe DiMaggio (1,537)
RF Babe Ruth (2,204)
BENCH: Hank Aaron (2,297); Ty Cobb (1,959);
      Stan Musial (1,951); Hank Greenberg
      (1,276); Jimmie Foxx (1,922); Willie
      Mays (1,903); Mel Ott (1,860)

Ah, a controversy brews in these selections. But first, let me explain my method of selection. Two criteria were most important: lifetime average RBIs per game and total lifetime RBIs. Another, though less important consideration: outstanding single-season RBI mark.

I am looking for a combination of efficiency and actual productivity. Therefore, for example, though Hank Aaron is number one in lifetime RBIs, he is not on our first team because Ruth's efficiency (.88 RBIs per game) is the fifth-best mark of all time—and he's only 93 total RBIs behind Aaron—while Hank's efficiency is twenty-fourth (.70). Sorry Hank.

Hank Greenberg is another guy who almost made this team. Hank's efficiency (.92) is tied for the top all-time spot (with Gehrig and old-timer Sam Thompson), but he had nearly 600 less lifetime RBIs than Ted Williams— that's six 100-RBI seasons *less*. Nod to Teddy. Conversely, though Ty Cobb actually had more lifetime RBIs than Williams, he is not in the top thirty-five in efficiency and Williams is eighth.

Some more close calls. Willie Mays had 366 more RBIs than Joe D., but the latter is fourth in all-time efficiency (.89) and Willie isn't in the top thirty-five. And hats off to Hack Wilson whose 190 ribbies for the 1930 Cubs is an all-time record—and one that may last forever.

Yogi's nod behind the plate was close over Bill Dickey, Gabby Harnett, the old-time Cub great, Johnny Bench, and Roy Campanella. Campy might have been the winner if not for a combination of bigotry and bad luck. Campy didn't get into the majors until he was twenty-seven, by which time Yogi already had 557 RBIs. Ten years later his career was over due to a terrible automobile accident. Campy's efficiency makes him nineteenth on the all-time list, the best of all the catchers.

Honus Wagner's total of 1,732 is twelfth all time, and 308 better than Senator and Red Sox great Joe Cronin. Eddie Mathews, with a .61 rate and 1,453 total RBIs, is our wonderful third baseman. Give Cub great Ron Santo an honorable mention (.59; 1,331); if some of his teammates had been on base more frequently, Ron would have done a lot better. Oh well. (For Harmon Killebrew supporters: though he topped Mathews in both home runs and RBIs, Killebrew played only four seasons as a full-time hot corner operator—792 games, approximately one third Mathews' total). Mike Schmidt and Graig Nettles are today's best.

Hornsby was the winner at second over greats Charlie Gehringer, Bobby Doerr, Frankie Frisch, and Tony Lazzeri.

A couple of pitchers have some amazing RBI stats besides the Red Sox and Yankee great Ruffing—who had the exact number of victories, 273, as he had ribbies. Wes Ferrell hit .347 for the 1935 Red Sox with 52 hits and 32 RBIs, and ended up with 208 career RBIs. Tony Cloninger, who appeared primarily with Milwaukee and Atlanta in the sixties, had 9 RBIs on July 3, 1966, while mashing 2 grand-slam home runs. His lifetime marks were 11 homers and 67 RBIs with a .192 batting average. Tony's career ERA was 4.07, so he knew something about giving up homers.

Boy, Lou Gehrig was a good baseball player. It seems like he's first, second, or third in practically everything.

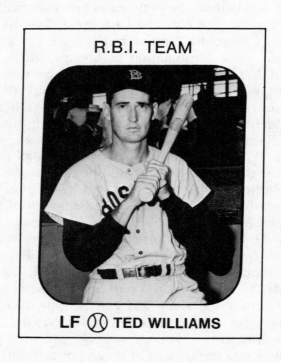

R.B.I. TEAM

LF ○ TED WILLIAMS

THE ITALIAN TEAM

P   Vic Raschi; Sal Maglie; Johnny Antonelli
C   Yogi Berra
1B   Joe Torre
2B   Tony Lazzeri
3B   Ron Santo
SS   Phil Rizzuto
LF   Tony Conigliaro
CF   Joe DiMaggio
RF   Rocky Colavito
BENCH: Dolph Camilli; Ernie Lombardi; Cookie Lavagetto; Dom DiMaggio; Billy Martin; Sal Bando; Jim Fregosi; Carl Furillo; Rico Petrocelli; Phil Carvaretta; Dave Righetti; Lee Mazzilli; Joe Pepitone; Gary Gaetti; John Castino; Ralph Branca; Gene Tenace
MANAGER: Tommy LaSorda

This is an awfully good team, but isn't it odd that no current athletes of Italian descent can make this starting team? Where are all the good Italian athletes putting their energies? Computer games? Good grief.

Slightly less odd is the dearth of Italian pitchers. Sure, Raschi and Maglie were very good, but after that there's quite a fall-off to Antonelli and Branca. Of course, if Dave Righetti, the AL Rookie of the Year in 1981, keeps it going the staff will be in good shape. Maybe if Joe Sambito's arm gets better he'll make this team in the next edition. It's up to baseball-loving fans of Italian descent to get their kids away from video games and out onto the field shagging flies and taking a hundred cuts a day. Let's go!

Vic Raschi, one of the fiercest competitors ever to brush back a batter, owns the fifth-best winning percentage in history at .667 (132–66). In a money game he's our "Italian Stallion." Sal the Barber's right there too, with the ninth-best winning percentage of .657 (119–62) and a temperament to match Raschi's. Antonelli was 21–7 with a 2.30 ERA and 6 shutouts in 1954, which ain't too shabby; we'll bring him in if the older guys foul up.

Yogi Berra was the easy choice at catcher. Only Johnny Bench has hit more homers from the catcher's spot. Many forget that in addition to power (358 HRs), Yogi hit for average too, ending up at .285, despite his habit of swinging at anything within three feet of the plate.

Joe Torre won over two other excellent first basemen, Dolph Camilli and Phil Cavaretta of the Dodgers and Cubs respectively. The NL MVP in 1971, after eschewing spaghetti and dropping fifty pounds, Torre was a lifetime .297 hitter with 252 homers. In 1971 he hit .363 with 24 HRs and 137 RBIs. We love ya, Joe.

Tony Lazzeri made his reputation primarily with the mighty Yankees of the late twenties and thirties. A lifetime .292 hitter, he had good power for a second baseman, with 178 career home runs. Tony's backup at second is Billy Martin.

Ron Santo (342 HRs; 1,331 RBIs) was the winner over Sal Bando (242; 1,039) in a battle of excellent third sackers. Both have reputations as good fielders and cheerful, agreeable human beings.

At short, the "Scooter" was a comfortable choice over Rico Petrocelli, the Red Sox shortstop of the sixties and seventies. The latter still holds the AL record for homers by a SS with 40 (1969) but Rizzuto was a spectacular fielder, terrific base runner, and career .273 hitter. The MVP of the AL in 1950, Scooter wowed them with a .324 year and 200 hits.

The Italian Team possesses a powerful outfield in Colavito, DiMaggio, and Conigliaro. Rocky's reputation is a bit forgotten these days, but his 374 home runs topped DiMag's 361 and puts him in the top twenty-five. In addition, Colavito owned the most powerful throwing arm in baseball and was fun to watch at the plate because he pointed the end of his bat directly at the pitcher before assuming his stance—a habit that did not endear him to moundsmen.

DiMaggio may be the greatest player of all time. Enough said. Many forget that his younger brother Dom was excellent too—a fabulous center fielder with the Red Sox for eleven years who had a .298 career average. But Tony C. got the nod over Dom because of power. The youngest man in baseball history to reach 100 career homers, Conigliaro could hit and run and field. A frightening beaning ruined it all.

Pass the pasta, Mom. I wanna be a ball player.

ITALIAN TEAM

Bench ⚾ DOM DIMAGGIO

THE JEWISH TEAM

P   Sandy Koufax; Ken Holtzman; Steve
        Stone
C   Moe Berg
1B   Mike Epstein
2B   Rod Carew
3B   Al Rosen
SS   Andy Cohen
LF   Hank Greenberg
CF   Sid Gordon
RF   John Lowenstein
DH   Ron Blomberg
MANAGER: Norm Sherry
COACH: Jake Pitler
BENCH: Larry Sherry; Norm Larker; Cal Abrams;
        Larry Rosenthal; Richie Sheinblum; Mor-
        rie Arnovich; Buddy Myer; Goody Rosen;
        Johnny Kling; Harry Danning; Elliot Mad-
        dox
HONORABLE MENTION: Ed Levy

First, the author would like to extend his thanks to Rod
Carew for marrying a Jewish girl, converting, and filling
a badly needed roster spot at second base.

This team is a little thin on the mound, despite Koufax. Koufax and Holtzman and two days of rain? Of
course, Larry Sherry was an outstanding relief pitcher,
primarily with the Dodgers and Tigers (53–44, 3.67, 82
career saves).

Kenny Holtzman's best season was with the Oakland
A's in 1973 when they were World Series champs and he
went 21–13. His lifetime stats: 168–141 with a 3.44 ERA.
Ken had an unpleasant finish to his career with the Yankees. In one and a half seasons with Billy Martin he was
in exactly 23 games. Martin vocally derided Holtzman's

84

ability, a stunt he also pulled with Larry Gura, and simply wouldn't pitch him.

Moe Berg, the brilliant Princeton grad often described as the smartest man to ever play major league baseball, had a lifetime .244 batting average. Someone once said, "Berg can speak nine languages and can't hit a curve ball in any of them." Berg served with the OSS in World War II, later became a lawyer and gained fame in the 1950s by winning a considerable amount of money on a TV game show called "Information Please."

Mike Epstein's best year was with the Washington Senators in 1969 when he popped 30 homers, knocked in 99 runs, and hit .278. A Bronxite who went west to the University of California at Berkeley, where he was an outstanding college fullback, Epstein played in the 1972 World Series for Oakland and went 0 for 16. He ended up with a somewhat disappointing 130 homers and a .244 batting average. Big and strong at six-three and 230 pounds, Epstein called himself "Superjew."

Al Rosen was the AL MVP in 1953 when he hit 43 homers and had 145 RBIs. He had over 100 RBIs five times in his career, though his fielding left something to be desired. He retired after the 1956 season, though only thirty-two, because of a salary dispute with the Cleveland Indians, and ended up with 192 home runs and a .285 batting average.

Andy Cohen played three years with the New York Giants and the less said about him the better. Andy had a brother, Sid, who didn't pitch any better than Andy fielded.

Hank Greenberg is one of the greatest sluggers the game has ever known. In 1938 all Hank did was hit 58 home runs, knock in 146, and bat .315. Primarily a first baseman, Greenberg was also a more than adequate outfielder. His lifetime home run and RBI total (331, 1,276) would have been considerably higher but for war service, which cost him four and a half years in his prime.

At his peak, Sid Gordon was an excellent power-hitting outfielder with the New York Giants and Boston Braves. A lifetime .283 hitter, he had 202 home runs. His best year was with the Giants in 1948 when he hit 30 homers, knocked in 107 runs, and batted .299. Sid was one of those excellent players who never played in the World Series.

John Lowenstein, the excellent Oriole outfielder, does everything well, especially hitting in the clutch; a player who has improved year after year.

Ron Blomberg had one of the sweetest swings in the AL from 1969–78 but a series of crippling injuries, especially to his shoulder, prevented him from ever playing regularly. He had 200 at bats only four times in eight years. His lifetime .293 batting average is a bittersweet reminder of what could have been. At thirty it was over.

Ed Levy was born Edward Clarence Whitner and was not Jewish. Early in his thoroughly forgettable career his baseball employers declared their need for a "Jewish" ball player as a gate attraction. Ed Whitner became Ed Levy. Only in America.

It's a safe bet that the Italian team would clobber the Jewish team—unless Koufax could pitch every day.

Interestingly, the same fate that has befallen the Italians has struck the Jewish ball players as well: the disappearing-from-baseball act. Of the players on the entire Jewish team roster only Carew and Lowenstein are currently active.

THE BLACK TEAM

P   Bob Gibson; Fergie Jenkins;
Don Newcombe
C   Roy Campanella
1B   Willie McCovey
2B   Joe Morgan
3B   Jackie Robinson
SS   Ernie Banks
LF   Hank Aaron
CF   Willie Mays
RF   Frank Robinson
DH   Willie Stargell

BENCH: Lou Brock; Billy Williams; Elston Howard; Larry Doby; Reggie Jackson; Richie Allen; Maury Wills; Satchel Paige; Vida Blue; Eddie Murray; Jim Rice; George Foster; Joe Black

A surfeit of riches. My Aunt Sadie could manage this team to the world championship.

Every single player (except for Newcombe) on this starting team will be, or is, in the Hall of Fame.

The author is white. And green with envy.

87

THE UNDERRATED TEAM

P   Larry Gura; Ken Forsch
C   Gene Tenace
1B   Mike Hargrove
2B   Lou Whitaker
3B   Toby Harrah
SS   Bucky Dent
LF   José Cruz
CF   Amos Otis
RF   Oscar Gamble
DH   Cliff Johnson
MANAGER: Chuck Tanner
HONORABLE MENTION: Dave Rozema; Rupert Jones; Darrell Evans; Jim Gantner; Bob Watson; Tony Perez; Dickie Thon; Andre Thorton; Willie Upshaw; Bill Buckner; Gary Roenicke; Chris Chambliss; George Hendrick; Lloyd Moseby; Bill Madlock; Harold Baines

He's not big, he's not fast, and he's not loud; all Larry Gura does is get the job done. Now thirty-five years old, he has one of the best winning percentages in history (.607), always gives up less hits than innings pitched, and still seems to be improving. Ken Forsch is big but not fast, and that combination often gets a pitcher underestimated. But Ken has a 3.16 lifetime ERA, though his lifetime record is about .500—thanks to eleven years pitching for the Astros. Excellent control pitcher, durable too; at thirty-six still close to peak. California manager Gene Mauch, continuing the pattern of underrating Forsch, jumped motormouth media darling Tommy John ahead of him in the 1982 AL championship—and lost as a result.

Gene Tenace isn't pretty, isn't fast, isn't flashy, and

doesn't hit for average. All he does is knock in runs and hit home runs—consistently. Plus, he is usually among the league leaders in bases on balls—a decidedly un-flashy statistic. It is not a coincidence that Fury Gene (his real name) has played on six pennant winners.

Mike Hargrove is a lifetime .296 hitter and one of the best first basemen in baseball. He also has had the misfortune to play on bad teams in relatively small cities with little media coverage (Arlington, Texas; San Diego; Cleveland) and has thus largely escaped with his ano-nymity intact.

Lou Whitaker isn't spectacular, just excellent, and getting better. Lou led the AL second basemen in assists in 1981, has great range, and a rapidly improving bat.

Toby Harrah will never make anyone forget Brooks Robinson with the glove, but his "stone fingers" reputa-tion was earned at shortstop, and is undeserved for his play at third. Harrah hits for average with lots of power and often knocks in the few Indian teammates that do reach base ahead of him. Buried in Cleveland—but not forgotten.

A few years ago, to label Bucky Dent, the wealthy shortstop, "underrated" would have been silly. But since being banished to Texas by the wrong-headed Yankee front office his stock seems to have plummeted, for no good reason. The most consistent shortstop in baseball, Bucky is stubby and slow and incapable of doing any-thing with flair. Who cares? (And hats off to Dickie Thon, who Bucky just edged out at short. He is tough and smart, steals bases, and in 1983 even hit for power. By 1985 he will be baseball's best shortstop.)

José Cruz has been stuck in Houston for eight years, the worst hitter's park in the major leagues. An excel-lent, agressive outfielder, José steals bases (single-sea-son high of 44), knocks in runs (high of 91), and hits for average (.315 high) with lots of doubles. The Astrodome has broken a lot of spirits—but not José's.

Amos Otis plays too deep. Amos Otis shies away from hard-throwing right-handers. Amos Otis doesn't throw his body into outfield walls. So what? Year after year after year—for a total of thirteen—he has been one of the very best players in the game. He hits for average (.280), power (26 homers is his high), and in the clutch (over 75 RBIs six times). He steals bases, with a single season high of 52. He has an excellent throwing arm and always has one of the highest fielding averages in the game. If Amos Otis at age thirty-six wants to move his head back a little from some wild-throwing 100-mph pitcher it's fine by me. Except for the Nolan Ryan–Jim Fregosi deal, the stupidest trade the Mets have ever made was losing Amos Otis (for Joe Foy!). In fact, it might be the worst goof in baseball history. Keep on trucking, Amos.

Oscar Gamble has been incarcerated in The Bronx Zoo twice, for a total of five years. His home run rate is in the top ten of current major leaguers but he hasn't even had 200 at bats in a season since 1979. Gamble can run, throw, and field. Possessed of an unusually sunny disposition, even Oscar began to complain when the Yankees again buried him on the bench in 1983. He should keep complaining. Loudly.

I've heard some of the bizarre stories about Cliff Johnson too, but who with a combination of his big talent and small playing time wouldn't act up a bit? Another victim of the Astrodome (five long years), Johnson has one of the highest home run and RBI rates of any active player, yet he has had over 275 at bats exactly three times in his eleven-year career. Bill James in *The Baseball Extract* wonders what would have happened if Cliff Johnson had played in Fenway Park. Good God, there's no telling how many home runs Johnson would have hit. Cliff is a slow-talking, slow-moving Southerner who instead of quietly accepting his fate should have ranted, raved, gone out on strike, and generally caused big trouble until he got traded somewhere they would have put him on the field and let him do his job. Some combination of fate and executive or managerial stupidity have conspired to spoil what could have been a memorable career. Baseball can be a very weird game sometimes.

Chuck Tanner is smart, bold, and sensitive—the best manager in the major leagues.

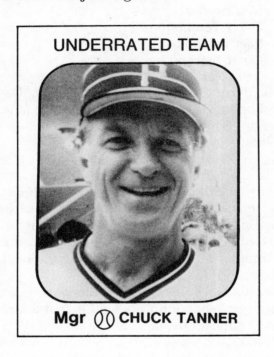

UNDERRATED TEAM

Mgr CHUCK TANNER

THE OVERRATED TEAM

P   Mike Norris; Dennis Eckersley
C   John Stearns
1B   Willie Aikens
2B   Johnny Evers
3B   Bob Horner
SS   Garry Templeton
LF   Ellis Valentine
CF   Omar Moreno
RF   Dave Parker
BENCH: Jerry Remy; Rabbit Maranville; Dave
        Lopes; George Foster; Caesar Cedeno
MANAGER: Billy Martin

Every other year Mike Norris has a good year. In 1982 it was bad. Consistency is everything in baseball, and Mike, who uncorks wild pitches regularly, is anything but consistent. Dennis Eckersley has very quietly become just another pitcher. Without the great fastball, he has insufficient guile to get by.

John Stearns can't throw, never hits with power, and never shuts up. What John does do is look more like a baseball than almost anyone.

Willie Aikens swings as hard as he can on every pitch anywhere near the plate. In addition, he makes Dave Kingman look like a Golden Glover.

Bob Horner can't even monitor his own weight without inducement. A classic example of statistics being misleading, Bob hits homers only in the friendly confines of the Braves' park, rarely gets the big hit, and is probably the worst third baseman in major league baseball.

Ellis Valentine, pardon the cliché, is a loser. Superbly gifted, he is in the process, for reasons known only to him, of utterly wasting those gifts. Speaking of wasting gifts, how about Garry Templeton, whose descent into mediocrity is as sad as it is unnecessary.

Omar Moreno is an Astro-turf player, perhaps the ultimate artificial surface outfielder. An excellent outfielder, one wonders whether natural turf with its less predictable hops would lessen his effectiveness. Be that as it may, Moreno is a lifetime .257 hitter with no power whatsoever, and a terrible career on-base percentage of .315. Valuable yes, outstanding, come on.

Dave Parker in right field? Who else? A man who has seen his game deteriorate as his waist line has expanded. Once a good outfielder, he has, perhaps, the worst range in baseball today. He is inconsistent and moody, traits that spell serious trouble in the sport of baseball.

Billy Martin is almost always excellent the first year he manages a team, good the second, and a disaster-in-the-making by the third.

Special Mention: Johnny Evers, second base. Evers is in the Hall of Fame because newspaperman Franklin Adams wrote an eight-line poem that appeared in the now-defunct *New York Evening Mail* that began:

These are the saddest of all possible words,
Tinker to Evers to Chance . . .

Johnny Evers was a lifetime .270 hitter (1902–17) in a period when most regulars batted .300. He averaged 30 RBIs a year and in eighteen years had 12 home runs. A good player certainly, but the idea that truly outstanding modern players like Gil Hodges, Rocky Colavito, and Phil Rizzuto aren't in the Hall and he is, is simply ludicrous.

THE BAD, BAD LUCK TEAM

P	Don Wilson; Francisco Barrios
C	Thurman Munson
1B	Harry Agganis
2B	Ken Hubbs
3B	Steve Macko
SS	Fritz Brickell
LF	Walt Bond
CF	Lyman Bostock
RF	Roberto Clemente

HONORARY CAPTAIN: Lou Gehrig

MANAGER: Gil Hodges; Ken Boyer; Fred Hutchinson

Somehow, when an athlete dies in his prime, for whatever reason, there is an added poignancy, as though the waste of such special physical vitality makes death even more unfair.

Some of the men above died valorously, some ignominiously. Accidents, disease, human frailty—whatever the cause, all died before their time.

If there is a lesson from this, perhaps Ronsard put it best:

> *Live now, believe me,*
> *Wait not till tomorrow*
> *Gather the roses of life today.*

THE SHORT TEAM

P   Bobby Shantz (5'6'')
      Clark Griffith (5'6'')
D   Yogi Berra (5'7½'')
1B   Steve Garvey (5'9'')
2B   Joe Morgan (5'7'')
3B   Rabbit Maranville (5'5'')
SS   Phil Rizzuto (5'6'')
LF   Wee Willie Keeler (5'4'')
CF   Al Bumbry (5'7'')
RF   Albie Pearson (5'5'')
PH   Eddie Gaedel (3'7'')
BENCH: Walt "No Neck" Williams (5'6''); Ernie Oravez (5'4''); Fred Patek (5'5''); Hugh Nicol (5'4''); Vic Davalillo (5'7''); Hack Wilson (5'6''); Onix Concepcion (5'6'')
MANAGER: Miller Huggins (5'4'')

I think no virtue goes with size.
      —Ralph Waldo Emerson

"Right on!" cries our team.

Pitchers are usually guys with slablike hands and shoulders the width of doorways. Bobby Shantz, weighing in at 139 pounds soaking wet, was MVP of the American League in 1952, when he won 24 games.

Yogi Berra is very short, but he is not small. Same goes for Morgan and Garvey. This lineup has some punch, make no mistake about that. Garvey, by the way, is by far the tallest guy here, with the largest forearms too; every other first baseman who ever played was six-three and weighed 215 pounds.

If Shantz stood on the home plate side of the pitcher's mound he would have no idea whether our short outfield was even on the field. Wave your arms, Albie!

Of these short guys, Berra, Griffith, and Keeler are in the Hall of Fame. Garvey and Morgan are certain to be there, and Rizzuto should be. Midget power.

Some people who you think are short, aren't: Billy Martin, Pee Wee Reese, Harvey Haddix, and Al Jackson.

One of the terrific things about baseball is that you don't have to be six-ten or weigh 285 pounds to play effectively. Baseball is still a game that is at human scale. It is not a freak show.

The author is five-feet-nine-inches tall.

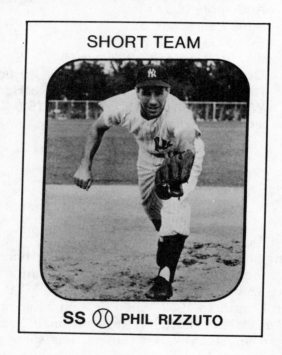

SHORT TEAM

SS PHIL RIZZUTO

THE TALL TEAM

P	Gene Conley (6'8")
	Tim Stoddard (6'8")
	Mike Smithson (6'8")
	J.R. Richard (6'8")
C	Fran Healy (6'5")
1B	Walt Bond (6'7")
2B	Jerry Lumpe (6'3")
3B	Danny Ainge (6'4")
SS	Bill Almon (6'3")
LF	Frank Howard (6'7")
CF	Dave Winfield (6'6")
RF	Dave Kingman (6'6")

Looking at the outfield on this team makes one feel very sorry for Dave Winfield. In fact, this entire team would probably give a manager plenty of extra gray hairs.

But gosh, yes, they're big. And big, we hasten to add, does not necessarily mean clumsy. Gene Conley was a pro basketball player. Tim Stoddard, Frank Howard, and Dave Winfield were excellent college basketball players on very good teams. Kingman and Healy were both outstanding high school players. A basketball coach for The Tall Team would probably say, "Let Danny shoot, the rest of you guys rebound."

Thank God for Jerry Lumpe—every other second baseman who ever played was five-eight. Lumpe, who played twelve years, was a better than adequate fielder with the Yankees, Tigers, and Kansas City A's, and was a career .268 hitter. In his time, badly underrated. Today, largely forgotten.

Walt Bond is worthy of comment, in that the sad-faced first baseman had such an odd career. In 1964 he hit 20 homers and had 85 RBIs with the woeful Houston

Astros. In 1965 he hit 7 home runs. In 1966 he played in the minors. This is called a precipitous decline.

Fran Healy was tall, fast, and graceful—qualities not normally associated with a catcher. Healy, an excellent defensive catcher, had over 200 at bats only twice in his nine-year career and responded with .276 and .252 averages, and even stole 16 bases in the latter of those two seasons. Quiet, intelligent, and self-effacing to a fault, he is one of those players who never got the chance his talent deserved. (His father, Francis, who is short, was also a major league catcher.)

Frank Howard, a "space-eating" center for the Ohio State basketball team of 1956–58, probably hit a baseball further and harder than anyone else in history. In 1968, while with the Washington Senators, he went on the hottest home run tear in baseball history: over six games, and in 20 official at bats, Frank belted 10 home runs.

The short team would beat the tall team.

THE WORLD SERIES TEAM

P   Whitey Ford; Bob Gibson; Sandy Koufax
C   Yogi Berra
1B   Lou Gehrig
2B   Frankie Frisch
3B   Pepper Martin
SS   Pee Wee Reese
LF   Lou Brock
CF   Mickey Mantle
RF   Babe Ruth
MANAGER: Casey Stengel

Since the Yankees have been in thirty-two World Series, sixteen more Series appearances than the runner-up Dodgers, the team's players tend to dominate Series statistics. This probably figures, since they had to have had lots of good players to get into so many World Series. And since they won twenty-two of those thirty-two Series, those players had to have performed well, too.

For you Yankee-haters out there, The World Series Team will not be your favorite chapter. Give it a quick glance and move on.

For the less-emotional Yankee loathers, and other baseball fans, facts are facts. Whitey Ford, speaking of facts, is first in strikeouts, games, wins, and second in shutouts in Series history. Smiling Bob Gibson snarled BBs past aghast batsmen at a record rate, striking out 10.22 batters for every game he pitched, the best ever. Sandy Koufax is second in K rate at 9.63 and fifth in ERA at .95. In 1963 Koufax, who had gone 25–5 for the season and was as close to invincible as any pitcher will probably ever get, opened the Series by striking out 15 Yankees, breaking Carl Erskine's 1953 record of 14, also set against New York. The Dodgers swept in four. In 1968 Bob Gibson went Koufax two better, striking out 17 Detroit Tigers in the Series opener and besting 31-game winner Denny McLain. (Oddly, Gibson and McLain, who had both won their league's Cy Young and MVP awards, were overshadowed in the Series by rotund Mickey Lolich, who won 3 games, including the final.)

Yogi Berra is first in all-time Series games, at bats, and hits, second in total bases, RBIs (39), runs (41), and doubles, and third in homers (12) and bases on balls. Lou Gehrig has the third-highest slugging percentage in Series history (.731 behind Jackson and Ruth), is third in RBIs (35), in the top five in triples, homers, home run percentage, runs, and bases on balls, and hit .361.

Frankie Frisch hit .376, leads in doubles, is fifth in stolen bases, and fielded superbly in eight Series. He gets the nod in a close contest with Billy Martin, who hit .333 in Series competition—80 points higher than his lifetime average. When it came to "gearing-up" time, Martin was always ready, a mediocre player who drove himself to excellence.

Pepper Martin is the all-time Series leader in batting average at .418. Martin batted .500 in the 1931 Series, stole 5 bases, made a game-saving catch to end the seventh contest, and became an instant national hero.

Pee Wee Reese was a close winner over his contemporary, Phil Rizzuto, at shortstop. Reese is fifth on the all-time Series hit parade with 46 and the Scooter only hit .246 in Series competition.

Lou Brock is first in Series stolen bases, which isn't very surprising; his batting average of .391 is second all-time and a bit more of a surprise, but his slugging percentage is .655, fifth all-time and very surprising. In the '67 Series Brock hit .414 and in the '68 Series went .464 with 3 doubles, 1 triple, and 2 homers. It wasn't Lou's fault the Tigers won.

Mickey Mantle is first in home runs (18), RBIs (40), total bases, bases on balls, and runs (42). An easy choice.

Babe Ruth gets the nod in a very close contest with Reggie Jackson. Ruth is tops in home run percentage, second in homers, slugging average, and bases on balls, third in total bases and runs to go along with a .326 batting average. Reggie's record is also admirable: first in slugging average at .767 and second in home run percentage to go with a .360 average. Reggie hit 3 homers—each on the first pitch—in the '77 Series final game, tying Ruth's record, which the latter did twice.

Odd Fact Department: Babe Ruth, the pitcher, is third on the Series all-time ERA list, ahead of Koufax, Ford, and Gibson.

WORLD SERIES TEAM

Mgr ⓧ CASEY STENGEL

THE DISAGREEABLE TEAM

(Disagreeable: Hard to get along with; quarrelsome.)

P	Steve Carlton; Mike Marshall
C	Thurman Munson
1B	Dave Kingman
2B	Rogers Hornsby
3B	George Brett
SS	Garry Templeton
LF	Ted Williams
CF	Ty Cobb
RF	Caesar Cedeno

MANAGER: Billy Martin
OWNER: George Steinbrenner
OWNER EMERITUS: Charlie Finley

The first observation an observant person might make about this team is that it is made up predominantly of modern-day ball players. This says something about money not buying happiness.

Speaking of money makes one wonder whether there is a connection between disagreeableness and penuriousness. Dave Kingman, as grim and unpleasant a man as has ever played the grand old game, has a reputation for extreme frugality. Legend has it that Mr. Kingman sold a handsome, expensive boat to his manager, George Bamberger, just after the completion of the 1982 season. When George went to pick up the boat he discovered the gas tanks dead empty.

Kingman, of course, isn't all bad. He played a funny practical joke on a female reporter who was attempting an interview after a rare Met victory. Dave, clearly in high spirits, dumped ice water over her head. (Later, it turned out this wasn't a practical joke after all, but Dave's way of making an intellectual argument: Women shouldn't be allowed in the locker rooms of major league baseball teams. The Supreme Court of the United States States disagrees with Dave on this point.)

If disagreeable means quarrelsome then Billy Martin, Leo Durocher and Earl Weaver notwithstanding, is clearly the overwhelming choice as manager of this team. There are, of course, legions of Martin fighting stories. Billy beating up bouncers, beating up marshmallow salesmen, beating up sailors, even beating up his own ball players on several occasions.

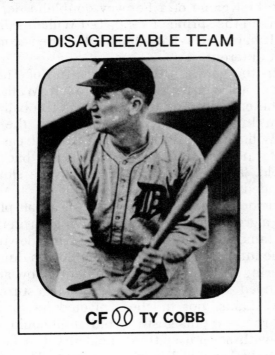

DISAGREEABLE TEAM

CF ⚾ TY COBB

The stories of these pugilistic triumphs usually come out sounding like classic tales of the scrappy little guy with the big heart overcoming long odds to defeat Goliath-like foes. Actually, they are stories of a trained boxer punching out amateurish, hopelessly overmatched opponents. Bob Grim, an ex-Yankee pitcher, once saw Martin working out on a speed punching bag and was awed by what he saw: "He could make that baby talk. Not just left and right, but he could hit it with his elbows, or even his head. I don't think he wanted people to know what he could do with his fists. He never talked about it."

And no wonder—it would spoil a nice little myth. Instead of an underdog, Martin was almost a sure winner, and he knew it. Stacked deck. Billy Martin, despite a positive public image, is not a very nice person.

In the first game of a Fenway doubleheader against the Tigers in the spring of 1950, Ted Williams dropped a fly ball. It happens. What happened in the second game was a bit different.

Late in the game, with the bases full of Tigers, Vic Wertz sent a line drive slicing out to left. Williams misplayed the ball, heading for the line as the ball skipped past him into the corner. That's when the trouble started. Williams literally loped after the ball, casually retrieved it, and tossed a looping, lazy throw back toward the infield. Three runners scored and the slow-footed Wertz ended up on third.

The incident was a rare example of a ball player, in this case a great ball player, simply giving up on the field. And the fans, naturally, booed him up and down. At the end of the inning Williams ran to the Boston dugout. Before entering he stopped, and with bent elbow and open palm, flipped a universally understood gesture to the crowd. Williams, not finished, pivoted left and right, carefully repeating his gesture so that all could see.

Along with several spitting incidents (on fans) this story assured Terrible Teddy's election to The Disagreeable Team. It was not a difficult decision.

Garry Templeton's comment one year on his selection to the NL All-Star team says quite a bit about him: "If I ain't startin', I ain't goin'." Garry has had trouble with his choice of sign language too.

Rogers Hornsby, one of the game's greatest hitters, a man who batted over .400 three times, was almost universally disliked. Despite his greatness he was traded an amazing seven times during an era when trades, especially of stars, were rare. Hornsby also managed ten teams, in the majors and minors, prompting Jimmy Breslin to speculate that Hornsby must have been fired "fifty" times.

Hornsby's trouble was that not only was he constantly disagreeable, but very loud about it. Two examples: In 1961, when Roger Maris was doing the unthinkable walking in the home run footsteps of Babe Ruth, Hornsby, a friend of Ruth's, called Maris a "punk" and a "bush leaguer." As a Met coach in 1962, Hornsby described the team to the press as "garbage," so bad that they "frighten you." This did not make the ball players, human beings one and all, feel very good.

Caesar Cedeño is ethically abhorrent to the author. This position has everything to do with the shooting death of a young woman in a motel room.

Steve Carlton is utterly silent to the press, but popular with his teammates. If he were merely taciturn he wouldn't be on this team. But he won't say a word, and that constitutes being "hard to get along with" and puts him on the disagreeable club.

Thurman Munson was similar to Carlton, again well liked by most of his fellow players, and almost universally disliked by the press. Munson's typical response to a question was profane and his anger seemed so genuine, and so close to the surface, that most reporters, physically intimidated, gave him a wide berth.

George Steinbrenner has done as much as anyone ever has, in nine short years, to cheapen and foul the game of baseball. His win-at-all-costs philosophy of baseball has seeped down to the fans to the point where victory is a requirement for a successful season and that anything less than a World Championship is cause for public apology. This attitude taken to its logical extreme would mean that every year the fans of twenty-five major league teams would have nothing to feel good about at the end of the season. If you're not a winner, then you are a loser. The destination is everything, the route nothing. It is a philosophy that is both repugnant and ultimately self-defeating.

Best of the worst? Undoubtedly George Brett. He had been a gentleman most of his career. Unfortunately, over the last couple of years there have been some changes in his demeanor. These changes included clubbing a reporter with a crutch, and smashing a photographers' camera. Welcome to the team, George. We hope to take you off in our next edition.

A final observation about The Disagreeable Team: Most of them were or are highly intelligent, clearly above the average of their peers, as well as being above-average players. Mike Marshall, for example, has a Ph.D—and the temperament of a first grader. Why intelligence makes for such disagreeableness I'll never know.

Maybe some intrepid soul should ask Dave Kingman's opinion. I'll pass.

THE FINANCIAL TEAM

P   Wes Stock; Gary Fortune
C   William Loan
1B   Norm Cash
2B   James Shilling
3B   Don Money
SS   Ernie Banks
LF   Reid Nichols
CF   Bobby Bonds
RF   Elmer Pence
BENCH: Woodrow Rich; Lester Sell; Jimmy Price; James Merchant
MANAGER: Harry Means

We see some interesting advertising opportunities here. How about Don Money for The Money Store? Bobby Bonds for E. F. Hutton?

Ernie Banks at Chase Manhattan has a nice ring to it.

IN-THEIR-FATHERS'-FOOTSTEPS

P	Steve Trout (Dizzy); Steve Narleski (Ray)
	Matt Keough (Marty)
C	Terry Kennedy (Bob)
1B	Bob Boone (Ray)
2B	Bump Wills (Maury)
3B	Roy Smalley (Roy)
SS	Dale Berra (Yogi)
LF	Buddy Bell (Gus)
CF	Terry Francona (Tito)
RF	Craig Landis (Jim)

To be eligible for this team you must be a current player whose dad played in the big leagues. That's why we don't have Keith Hernandez at first base—his father John played nine *minor* league seasons. Now for you purists we know very well that Bob Boone isn't a first baseman, but we gave him a quick call and he said, "If you need me, I'll try it." That's the spirit, Bob! (We reassured Boonie by reminding him that he started out in the minors as a first sacker, and even got into a game at that position as recently as 1978. "It's like riding a bike," we told him, "you don't forget.")

Of the fathers, Yogi and Maury Wills were clearly the best players, which isn't putting anybody down, since they were truly outstanding.

Dizzy Trout was an excellent pitcher, primarily with the Tigers between 1939–52, who won 20 games twice and ended up with 170 wins and an ERA of 3.23. Ray Narleski wasn't of Dizzy's caliber but his career record was 43–33 with a respectable 3.60 ERA. Plus *his* father, Bill, played two seasons for the Red Sox. Practically a Narleski dynasty.

Matt Keough, the best pitcher of the sons, can be proud of his father Marty who was a fine outfielder, though a light hitter, with the Red Sox and Reds through eleven big-league seasons. Marty's younger brother, Joe, played six seasons too, sharing the good-field, light-hit label.

Bob Kennedy, an outfielder and third baseman, played sixteen big-league seasons (1939–57) with a season high .291 with the 1950 Indians. He later managed the Cubs and Oakland A's, and is currently an Astro executive. Terry, a good-hitting catcher, looks like he's going to be better than Dad. Sorry, Pop.

Ray Boone, the agreeable Bob's father, was a very good infielder, primarily in the American League, for thirteen years (1948–60). A lifetime .275 hitter, he led the AL in RBIs in 1955 with 116, had a single-season high of 26 homers in 1953, and a career total of 151. A versatile and talented player, much like his widely admired son.

Bump Wills and Dale Berra had tough acts to follow, and have followed them very successfully. Berra took over the Pirate shortstop job full-time in 1982 and won many supporters with his steady fielding and clutch hitting (.263 with 61 RBIs). Wills, Bump that is, has been a vastly underrated second baseman. A steady, if unspectacular fielder, Wills bounced back in 1982 from a subpar 1981, hitting .272 for the Cubs with 35 stolen bases.

Gus Bell was a power-hitting outfielder, primarily with the Cincinnati Reds, who hit 206 homers with a lifetime .281 average. Roy Smalley, father of Roy Smalley, was an excellent-fielding shortstop with a lifetime .227 average. In 1950 the light hitter amazed the league by ripping 21 home runs and knocking in 85 runs. Inexplicably, he never played a full season in his remaining eight years.

Buddy Bell is, I'm sure, secure enough to do some position shifting. At third Bell is simply outstanding, and, with Mike Schmidt and Graig Nettles, one of the three best in the business. In left field, with pointers from Dad, he'll be fine. Smalley played third and first in the Yankees' musical chairs 1983 season, as well as short, and had another quietly efficient season.

Jim Landis was one of the best outfielders in the AL between 1957 and 1967. His best year at the plate, with the White Sox in 1961, showed 22 home runs and a .283 average. The jury's still out on son Craig.

Tito Francona played for fifteen years (1956–70) and had his best season with the 1959 Indians when he hit .363 with 20 homers and 79 RBIs. He was an accomplished outfielder and first baseman who was popular with teammates and fans alike. Tito's son Terry is a very promising young player who went so wild in 1981 with Denver in Triple-A ball (.352) that the Expos were forced to bring him up in only his second professional season. Terry was college player of the year with the University of Arizona in 1980 and was hitting .321 in 1982 (41 games) before a serious leg injury ended his season. Despite a ponderous knee brace he came on strongly in 1983.

Many other major leaguers had fathers who toiled in the minors; among them are Larry Bowa (Paul), Mike Flanagan (Ed), Doug Flynn (Robert Douglas), Barry Foote (Amby), Rollie Fingers (George), Todd Cruz (Robert), Bruce Benedict (David), and Mike Caldwell (Ralph).

The lesson of all this has something to do with a scientist named Mendel and a field called genetics. Bob Boone went to an excellent university, Stanford, and graduated with a science degree; we suggest directing all inquiries to him, care of the California Angels. Thanks again, Bob.

THE BIZARRE BATTING STANCE TEAM

P   Hank Aguirre
C   Milt May
1B   Vic Power
2B   Dick McAuliffe
3B   Brian Downing
SS   Gil McDougald
LF   Rickey Henderson
CF   Mickey Rivers
RF   Jesus Alou
HONORABLE MENTION: Stan Musial; Mel Hall; Oscar Gamble; Leon Wagner; Elston Howard; Joe Morgan; Gene Woodling; Carl Yastrzemski (early); Rocky Colavito

The author hates it when some know-it-all looks you straight in the eye and says that Milt May's stance isn't really that weird because he gets his bat into "hitting position." So what? Who cares? We're not discussing hitting technique here, we're discussing batting *stances;* the way a hitter looks, at the plate, before the pitcher delivers the ball. Anyone who wants to talk about "hitting position" should call Charley Lau.

Milt May has a bizarre, weird, ridiculous-looking batting stance. And, that's that.

It would be impossible for our most gifted novelists to describe the stances of the players selected for this team, so I'm certainly not going to try. But here are some impressions of those stances I'd like to share.

Hank Aguirre's stance looked like a complete surrender. "I'll stand here, you throw the ball, I'll swing and miss, then go back to the dugout. Okay?" (Hank hit .085 lifetime, a fact noted elsewhere in this book but so absurd that it bears repeating.)

Vic Power's stance was a dare, a challenge. It irritated

111

enough pitchers that Vic was always ready to hit the dirt.

Dick McAuliffe probably couldn't sit still when he was in class, couldn't stand still when he was in the batter's box, and probably still can't sit or stand still.

BIZARRE STANCE TEAM

SS GIL McDOUGALD

Brian Downing, upon assuming his muscle-bound stance, appears to be going in two different directions at once: the left side looks late for the 5:05 out of Penn Station, the right side looks ready to pick up large, heavy objects and hoist them over his head. A definite split-personality.

McDougald's stance was described by Casey Stengel, his first big league manager, as "the lousiest-looking stance I've ever seen but he gets the job done so I can't say nothing." The tip of McDougald's bat drooped down toward the ground as the pitcher wound up—and an unlikelier technique you'll never see. With the "lousy" stance Gil hit .306 his first year and was the AL Rookie of the Year.

Rickey Henderson's stance makes him look Eddie Gaedel's height in the batter's box, which makes a lot of sense for a leadoff man. But with knees knocked together and feet twisted like a palsy victim there has never been a more awkward, downright worse-looking stance anytime, anywhere.

Mickey Rivers, feet moving, head bobbing (the two most heinous crimes in almost every batting instructor's rulebook) looks like a seventy-year-old man shuffling forward on an early-morning hot food line. Mickey is a .296 lifetime hitter, which shows what the author knows.

Jesus Alou looked more nervous in the batter's box than McAuliffe. Craning his neck like an egret while simultaneously twitching every other muscle in his body, he looked like a "before" model in a chiropractor's advertisement. Come to think of it, one wonders what Jesus' father did do for a living.

We hope lots of readers remember Rocky Colavito and Leon Wagner's stances. The Rock aimed his bat at the pitcher as though he were a mad Turk bent on assassination, and old Leon shook his tushie in ways that would have gotten him or anyone else arrested in the nineteenth century.

Good job, fellas.

THE FRANK TEAM

P   Frank Tanana; Frank Lary
C   Frank House
1B   Frank McCormick
2B   Frank Frisch
3B   Frank Malzone
SS   Frank White
LF   Frank Thomas
CF   Frank Robinson
RF   Frank Howard
BENCH EMERITUS: Frank Baker; Frank Chance
MANAGER: Herman Franks

Unfortunately, the author knows only too well that the Frank team would get their butts kicked by just about any other team one would care to put together.

There are some very odd characteristics about this Frank team. Except for Franks Robinson, Frisch, and White, this is an absurdly slow team. The Frank team doesn't really have a bad infield, but with Frank Howard and Frank Thomas next to him in the outfield, I would think that Frank Robinson might seriously consider changing his name. Don't do it, for God's sake!

F. Robby is the best player on this team and we're going to need every one of his 586 lifetime homers to keep us in ball games. Frankie Frisch, a Hall of Famer, is the second best player—and very good indeed.

I would like to immediately own up on the subject of playing Kansas City's fine second baseman, Frank White, out of position at short. It had to be done. I can't play Frank Duffy or Frank Taveras at short. I just can't. Don't make me do it. It's bad enough playing Frank House behind the plate, though he wasn't that bad a hitter at .248. But Frank House, you guessed it, was big as a house. He makes Frank Howard look quick. House's nickname was "Pig."

Once upon a time there was a very good pitcher named Frank Killen. Unfortunately he played around the time dinosaurs were disappearing from the earth and in good conscience I couldn't include him.

See, people named Frank are usually very honest.

The author is bitterly disappointed with the quality of this team. What a way to have to end a book.